FOOTBALL STORIES

FOOTBALL STORIES

BAD BOYS AND HARD MEN

Niall Edworthy

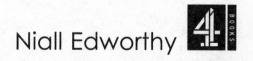

First published in 2002 by Channel 4 Books, an imprint of Pan Macmillan Ltd,
20 New Wharf Road, London N1 9RR, Basingstoke and Oxford.

Associated companies throughout the world.

www.macmillan.com

ISBN 0 7522 6480 X

9 8 7 6 5 4 3 2 1

A CIP catalogue record for this book is available from the British Library.

Designed by seagulls
Printed by Mackays of Chatham plc

MCAVENNIE

Executive Producer - Alan Clements
Producer/Director - Ross Wilson
Assistant Producer - Warwick Smith

MARADONA
Producer - Dermot Lavery
Director - Michael Hewitt

BEST
Producer - Michael Hewitt
Director - Dermot Lavery

PEARCE
endboard
Executive Producer - Sunandan Walia
Producer - Natasha Carlish
Director - Michael Clifford

CLOUGH Chrysalis
Television
Executive Producer - Tony Moss
Producer/Director - Andrew MacKenzie-Betty

JONES Chrysalis
Television
Executive Producer - Tony Moss
Producer - Alan Hurndall

FERGUSON

Executive Producer - Paul Murray
Producer/Director - Ross Wilson
Assistant Producer - Warwick Smith

CONTENTS

INTRODUCTION

The eight football characters profiled in this book have only one thing in common: they are not Gary Mabbutt. The former Tottenham and England defender is as unassuming, courteous and upstanding a figure you could hope to meet, outside of a Salvation Army coffee morning. We admired his modesty and his sportsmanship, but rarely did we spend evenings in the pub talking of little else but him. He was too clean cut, too honourable, too damned uncontroversial. A great man to have on your side but no 'side' to him. Just good honest Gary, an everyday guy who would happily water your plants, feed your cats and trim your hedge while you were on holiday.

This is not to say that the eight figures in this book lack admirable qualities, but rather that they have all seized our attention throughout their careers for entirely different reasons. They are outstanding football personalities who have brought some drama into the lives of those who follow the game – these days it's virtually impossible to be an interesting character without being controversial. We can work ourselves up into a froth of righteous indignation about the behaviour of some play-ers and managers, but at least they have managed to rouse our feel-ings, make us question our principles and stir up a debate about what is good or bad, right or wrong.

When we read reports of George Best falling down drunk in a pub, or being taken to hospital doubled up in agony, we're reminded that natural genius, wealth and public adoration are no guarantees of everlasting happiness. So too when Frank McAvennie appears before magistrates on drugs charges, just a few years after being snapped by the paparazzi living it up in Stringfellows nightclub. When Vinnie Jones bites a reporter's nose or threatens his neighbour, we're reminded that fame, fortune, a beautiful wife and a happy family are no guarantee of inner peace.

When Sir Alex Ferguson carpets his star player David Beckham for missing training to look after his sick child, you wonder what drives him. Is football really that important? When Maradona, the most gifted player of his generation, takes out an air rifle and opens fire on a group of journalists, you ask yourself what it must be like to have the world's media constantly hounding you. When Stuart Pearce steps up to take a crucial penalty, the eyes of the football world upon him, risking a soul-crushing repeat of a famous failure six years earlier, you question why it is that some people are more courageous than others. When Eric Cantona leaps into the crowd to attack an abusive fan, you wonder what it would be like to have to go to work and be expected to sit quietly and take the insults.

But when Gary Mabbutt appears on television for a post-match interview, we say, 'Seems like a nice guy, Mabbutt, doesn't he?' and then we get up and put the kettle on. Gary Mabbutt, however, is not an exception to a general rule. On the contrary, English Football is full of men like him, ordinary guys quietly going about their daily business of playing football. Just because we see them on television being cheered to the rafters by 40,000 fans, doesn't make them great characters. They're just good at football, in the same way that accountants have a flair for crunching numbers, or bricklayers have for laying bricks. Football is their gift, and football is more glamorous than accountancy and bricklaying, so we assume that those who work in it must necessarily be colourful and interesting. This is no more than a media illusion, the fantasy of celebrity, wishful thinking on the part of football fans who want their heroes on the pitch to be more than regular Joes.

Before the arrival of saturation television coverage and the explosion of general media interest in the game, footballers had mystique. We only saw them doing brilliant things on a football pitch on a Saturday afternoon, and then they disappeared down the tunnel whence they came. We could only *imagine* what they were like in their private lives, and young football fans were able to dream that their idols on the pitch were just as heroic off it. Now we know what they're like, and they're often no different from the rest of us. Not long ago there was a video produced which gave an insight into life 'behind-the scenes' with some Manchester United stars – in their dressing gowns, cooking fried eggs and doing humdrum tasks about the house. At a stroke, the air of mystery and magic that surrounded them on the football pitch disappeared.

Most footballers should be seen and not heard, and that's why we should cherish the game's characters, warts and all. Football would be far duller without them. The eight men featured in this book have all brought a little bit of excitement to people's lives, and for that we should be grateful.

BAD BOYS

ERIC CANTONA
A DEVIL OF A TEMPER

We all knew Eric Cantona came to English football with a bit of 'form'. But we had to wait until 25 January 1995 before it became apparent quite how far this awesomely temperamental Frenchman was prepared go in his efforts to bring some extra-curricular entertainment to his new public.

It was a routine sending off for the Manchester United forward, but as he made his familiar walk down the touchline with first claim on the best shower in the Selhurst Park changing room, the man they called 'Dieu' in one half of Manchester suddenly leapt in the air like a black-belt salmon and launched his studs towards the face of a Crystal Palace fan called Matthew Simmons. Wow. We rubbed our eyes and looked at our bottles when we saw the footage. Did that really happen? Fans invading pitches and attacking players we had seen before, but world-class players wading into the crowd – this was something very new and very exciting in football's roll-call of shame. Whatever next?

At first, there was an explosion of righteous outrage. Cantona would have to go was the near-universal response. But then the facts began to emerge. Cantona's 'victim' had taunted him with a tirade of disgusting abuse, including the suggestion that his mother was a prostitute and that the United forward had enjoyed sexual congress with her. The tone of indignation began to mellow in some quarters and one or two commentators even hailed the French hothead as a 'have-a-go hero'.

It was the latest major football scandal in a fifteenth-month period that gave us more off-pitch controversy than lawyers could have entertained in their wildest dreams. George Graham was sacked by Arsenal over the money-for-transfer 'bung' scandal. Paul Merson broke down in tears after confessing to his drink, drug and gambling problems. Dennis Wise went on trial charged with assaulting a taxi driver and damaging his vehicle. Bruce Grobbelaar was accused of fixing matches in return for cash while at Liverpool. And as if that wasn't enough, rioting English hooligans forced the abandonment of a friendly against the Republic of Ireland in Dublin. To top that bill, you had to have a bit of class – and England's favourite Frenchman had it by the bucket-load. The British have always loved a character and here was one who was brilliant at football – and, even better, he was playing for the team that was both the best supported and the most despised in the country.

Whatever your views on the morality of Eric 'See Red' Cantona's action, you had to admit that he provided a spectacular piece of football theatre at Selhurst Park on that cold January night. If Cantona had followed convention, he would have taken the abuse and walked calmly back to the changing room, muttering through gritted teeth

'I am a role model for young children, I am a role model for young chil-dren, keep a lid on it Eric, you're a big scary French volcano, deep breaths, deep breaths...'

'But où est le fun in that?' you could almost see him asking himself before springing into the front row like Bruce Lee. No one looked more surprised by the Frenchman's flight into the Selhurst Park public than Simmons himself. In fact, he seemed perfectly appalled by Cantona's behaviour. I mean, what on earth was the world coming to when you could no longer go to a football match and call someone's mother 'a f**king whore', without getting a mouthful of studs? Honestly.

Luckily for Cantona, his tormentor turned out not to be, say, a loveable old war veteran who instantly won the public's sympathy. Au contraire. Simmons, it turned out, had a bit of 'form' of his own. He was a petty criminal who, a few years earlier, had pleaded guilty to attacking a petrol station attendant with a spanner. Simmons's shady past would prove to be Eric's salvation. At first, the general consensus was that the Football Association would definitely hand the Frenchman a lengthy ban – possibly even for life. There were fears that if and once he returned, some fans would try extra hard to wind him up and Eric would be forced to spend most of his Saturday afternoons showing off his martial arts skills to – and on – the less sympathetic elements of the footballing public.

At the subsequent court case in Croydon, he arrived to be greeted with a chant of 'Going down! Going down!' from a small cluster of locals, presumably Palace fans. Inside, a stream of witnesses told the magistrate they had heard Simmons's vile tirade of abuse. To sniggers in the public gallery, Simmons denied he had used any such industrial language but had merely said to Cantona as he walked past: 'Off you go for an early shower.'

To the relief of his foreign legion of fans, Eric escaped a jail sentence and was given 120 hours of community service, which he fulfilled by teaching football to youngsters in the Greater Manchester area. The FA banned him for seven months, meaning he missed the end of the 1994/95 season and the first two months of the next. But the Cantona–Simmons show was to run for a little while yet. At a press conference after his court case, Cantona opened his mouth to speak just once, but what came out ensured his eternal place in the pantheon of football oddballs. 'When the seagulls follow the trawlers, they do it because they think sardines will be thrown into the sea,' he said in heavily accented English, squirming in his seat and his smart grey jacket. 'Thank you', he added and then got up and left the room. Fantastic stuff Eric, but what did it mean? Eric looked as embarrassed as anyone as he forced out his little slice of esoteric philosophy, concentrating intensely on not confusing his trawlers with his seagulls. Was this a lesser-known quote from Voltaire or Descartes, or was this an original work by Cantona himself? There was laughter and confusion among the assembled press corps but, damned fools, they didn't realize that the joke was actually on them. No one in the room understood what he meant, but after several days of hard work by the nation's amateur code-breakers and cryptologists, it was widely accepted that Eric was having a pop at the media – Eric being the trawler, the press being the seagulls and the sardines being Eric's 'bon mots'. One-nil Cantona.

At his own trial for threatening behaviour, Simmons put on such a show that big Eric, had he been there, would surely have risen to his feet and applauded. It was courtroom drama at its best. On being found guilty, Simmons jumped over a table towards lawyer Jeffery McCann, shouting, 'I am innocent. I swear on the holy bible!' There was, however, little sympathy for the Croydon One in court that day. Six officers dragged him off the lawyer and he was forced to pay a hefty fine, was banned from all football grounds for a year and jailed for seven days for contempt of court, although in the event, he was let out after one night. That, sadly for the nation's journalists, was the end of the story. Cantona returned to Manchester United and helped them to the most successful period in their history.

Far from seeing his popularity plummet after the incident, Cantona's stock rose sharply with the public and marketing people alike. A poll by a holiday operator found that over 40 per cent of men would rather go on holiday with the flying Frenchman than with Claudia Schiffer. He even appeared in an advert calling for an end to racist abuse. Not every-one, however, was grovelling at the feet of Le Roi. Brian Clough, no stranger himself to dishing out physical punishment to errant fans, was one of the loudest critics, calling for him to be thrown out of the English game. Clough, an entirely different type of maverick to Cantona, felt the Frenchman had overstepped the boundaries of acceptable rogue behav-iour. He likened Cantona's transgression to that of the fans he once cuffed for storming the pitch at Nottingham Forest's City Ground. 'He went somewhere he shouldn't have been,' said Clough. 'He should have walked around the track, had a shower, put on his smart French designer clothes and waited to get on the coach. There's something wrong with the man.'

In October, Cantona returned to action in style, scoring a penalty and setting up a goal in United's 2-2 draw at Liverpool. By the end of the season he had been voted Player of the Year by the country's foot-ball writers. At the award ceremony he took the opportunity to bless us with some more of his arcane wisdom. 'Some criticism means nothing and I compare it to a toilet,' he said. '"Screw them," I think.

It has been a long year, but a beautiful one.' That season United completed the double with a cup final victory over old rivals Liverpool, with you-know-who scoring the only goal of a dreadful contest. As he walked up Wembley's famous thirty-nine steps to collect the trophy, there was an anxious moment that must have tested the Frenchman's famously meagre patience to the limit. A group of Liverpool fans spat at him and hurled a volley of abuse. It was a hairy moment for all who held Cantona's best interests at heart, as he paused momentarily, presumably weighing up the risks of retaliation, before wiping away the spit and walking on.

Cantona certainly showed a far greater maturity following his return from the ban and United's current crop of world-class players, especially David Beckham, talk of him only in the most reverential of tones. Most commentators agree that without Cantona, United would probably never have enjoyed the success that they did in the mid-1990s, which generated a powerful momentum that saw them carrying all before them in the ensuing years.

• • •

The video footage of his early career in France becomes almost comic as you watch Cantona plumb depths of truly outstanding delinquency. It remains a wonder that the French authorities tolerated the 'enfant terrible' for so long. Watching him hurl shirts and balls, punching team-mates, stamping on opponents and insulting Henri Michel – the then national manager – it seems incredible that the man they called 'Le Brat' avoided being institutionalized, let alone escape a life ban from football.

Cantona grew up in Marseille, the poorer suburbs of which are amongst the toughest in France. 'He virtually lived in a cave with his family when he was much younger and that, of course, has a lot to do with his attitudes and various postures later on,' says football journalist Brian Glanville.

The man who first recognized Cantona's potential as a world-class footballer was Guy Roux, the coach at Auxerre for over thirty years and a living institution in French football. Roux, now well into his sixties, has almost single-handedly transformed the small provincial club into one of the country's top teams. Rarely has he spent more than two consecutive days away from a football pitch, but towards the end of 2001 his almost obsessive commitment to the his job led to a heart scare not long after his fellow Frenchman, Liverpool manager Gérard Houllier, underwent eleven hours of emergency surgery after collapsing in the Anfield dressing room. Doctors advised Roux to take a long rest from the game, but within weeks he was back in his office, wearing his familiar tatty tracksuit and woolly cap.

Roux has dedicated his working life to unearthing and nurturing football talent. When he is not on the training ground or in his office, Roux likes to drive around the Burgundy countryside watching local games and dropping into bars and nightclubs to make sure none of his players are out partying. 'Monsieur' Roux is said to have the eye and memory of a horse trader when it comes to footballers and the key to his success has been the quality of his football academy – the academy where Eric Cantona began his career at the age of fifteen.

'No, fourteen and a half to be precise,' says Roux. 'I remember his first day here very well. It was during a trial camp and he was so good that I immediately took him out of his age group and brought him to play with the professionals, in a seven-a-side match. He already had everything: the technical talent, the vision and this way of doing things with no apparent effort.

'He had interest from bigger clubs, but he chose to join Auxerre and he told me the reason why much later – because I had given him a club jersey. Eric is a very sensitive and faithful person. He was only seventeen years old when he made his debut in the first division and he was already the character that England would get to know so well. He was even wilder in many ways, like young men can be. At that time he was very volatile and he would have incredible tantrums when he thought something was unfair.'

Daniel Rolland, who has been in charge of the Auxerre youth academy since the mid-1970s, said Cantona's eruptions of rage were a common event, but were always born out of his fierce will to win. 'Eric hated losing so much that even in training he used to lose his temper. I had to calm him down many times when he was playing with the juniors because he was so agitated. He was in a team full of big personalities, two-thirds of whom went on to become full professionals. Among them were Basile Boli and Lionnel Charbonnier, who both played for France, and William Prunier, who had a brief spell at Manchester United.

'Our changing room at that time was very lively and extremely competitive, but the spirit was great. We won the two main trophies, the Gambardella Cup, the main youth competition and the amateur league. I remember well the final of the Gambardella Cup against Montpellier where Laurent Blanc was the number 10. Eric had had a bad semi-final because he was also playing with the pros at this time. But he set his mind on the final and had a terrific game, scoring a hat trick. It says a lot about the kind of competitor he was becoming – he has always been there for the big events.

'Eric told me not long ago that he has great memories of this period,' says Rolland. 'I can still remember when he arrived at the academy. He was quite a spindly kid, nothing like as powerful as he became later. He knew he had to work on his physique, but he was never afraid of hard training. Technically, however, he had everything. Andrej Szarmach, a great Polish striker who was playing for us at that time, immediately picked him out from the rest as a player to watch. We knew that he was going to become a very good professional, but exactly how good we couldn't say because we had worries about his mental stability and I was really upset by what he had to go through after he left Auxerre for Marseille.'

Rolland and Roux are too loyal to be drawn on the details, but some of his team-mates have painful memories of Cantona's eruptions of temper. One of them, Bruno Martini, the Auxerre goalkeeper who would later play for France, made the mistake of asking Cantona to help move the goalposts on the training pitch – in a tone of voice to which the striker took violent exception. Cantona's response was unequivocal. He punched him on the nose.

Martini was not the first and by no means the last player to experience Cantona's rage. Speaking before a match against Nantes in April 1988, Cantona explained to the assembled media how much he loved the beautiful style of football played by Nantes. But in the match itself Cantona had obvious difficulty in expressing his admiration. The Nantes central defender Michel der Zakarian, one of the hard men of French football, had marked Cantona out of the game using every trick he knew, fair or foul. Cantona was not amused, but he waited before choosing his moment. Der Zakarian was running with the ball along the touch line when Cantona, sprinting at full pelt, launched into him with a high, two-footed, studs-up tackle that sent the Nantes player crashing into the advertising boards with a broken leg. Cantona received a red card but afterwards he refused to express even the slightest hint of remorse. Au contraire. In his mind, he had been right, simply administering natural justice to a man who had dared to trespass against him.

'I had to spend a lot time explaining certain things which were not obvious to him,' says Roux. 'But he accepted my authority and despite his fits of anger, he had great friends in the team because he was so generous. Eric has a very big heart.'

Roux took a paternal as well as a professional interest in the young Cantona. 'During the autumn of 1987, I began to notice that he would vanish straight after all our home matches,' he says. 'I discovered that he had fallen in love with a young woman who was studying literature in Aix-en-Provence and living in Martigues. Every other Saturday night, he would get into his little Renault 5 and drive for six or seven hours to be with her. I said to myself, "One of these days we are going to find Eric on the side of the motorway, injured or killed," so I decided to take action and contacted the local club Martigues, then playing in the second division. I said to Eric: "Listen, I'm going to send you on loan to Martigues for the winter. Enjoy it. You will come back to Auxerre in April, but only come back married – not alone", and that's what he did. He returned in the spring with Isabelle, now his wife.'

Cantona has never forgotten Roux's kindness and talks of his time at Auxerre with a fondness that is conspicuously absent from his feelings for the rest of French football. 'Eric always has nice things to say about his days in Auxerre and I think we are the only club in France that he actually likes,' says Roux. 'When he was back in town to promote one of his films he sought me out to invite me to dinner with his son. To me, that's Eric. He is a big personality: generous, passionate, proud, immensely talented and very hard working too. Eric is the Balzac of French football.'

Roux says he was saddened and angered by what happened to Cantona after his transfer in 1988 to Olympique Marseille for a new French record of £2.3 million. The move made sense at the time: Marseille, his home town, was the biggest club in France, and Cantona was the country's rising star. He won national acclaim after scoring on his debut for France in a victory over mighty Germany and his transfer to Marseille was the big football story of the summer. Cantona, the hottest young property in French football, would be teaming up with Jean-Pierre Papin, one of the best strikers in the world. The pair were entirely different characters away from the pitch, but also on it: Papin the whippety poacher and Cantona the imperious big game hunter. The two instantly developed a powerful, symbiotic relationship when playing for their country and even though France generally under-performed during Cantona's period in the team (he played forty-three times for his country, scoring nineteen goals), he and 'JPP' were always a potent threat.

But the success of this partnership was not repeated at Marseille, where Cantona very quickly fell out of favour with Bernard Tapie, the controversial and dictatorial owner. Tapie, a flamboyant multi-millionaire and future minister in François Mitterand's government, dominated every aspect of life at France's biggest club. Cantona particularly hated the way that Tapie interfered at every level, often pulling rank on the team coach Gérard Gili.

Tapie was the central figure in a scandal that shook French politics as well as French football in the early 1990s. Convicted of bribing players to throw a match against Marseille, he was sent to jail for eight months. No one enjoyed Tapie's fall from grace more than Cantona, and while he was at Manchester United he liked to taunt Tapie by making jokes to French reporters about the manner in which Marseille had won its cup and trophies.

Tapie was a contentious figure long before these scandals hit the headlines and he would not tolerate any disobedience in those who played or worked for him. In Eric Cantona, he had bought the walking, breathing embodiment of surly insubordination and the two headstrong personalities couldn't stand each other. 'It was very unfortunate that Eric went to Marseille, where he refused to conform to the Tapie regime,' says Roux. 'It became a vicious circle as his temperament often got the better of him and the reaction of many people involved in French football forced him down a kind of dead end. There was a mutual lack of understanding and he could not stand it for long as referees started to target him.'

Cantona spent less than six months at Marseille, playing just twenty-two games, before two events gave Tapie the perfect excuse to offload his troublesome new recruit. After a match against Strasbourg early in the 1988 season Cantona, talking live on television, described the French national coach Henri Michel as 'un sac de merde' ('a bag of shit') after being left out of the squad. Then, in January 1989 during what was meant to be a friendly match at Sedan, Cantona exploded in a fit of pique more suited to the playground. Taunted by the local supporters from the opening whistle and increasingly frustrated by the referee's decisions, Cantona stormed off the pitch, ripping off his Marseille shirt and throwing it to the ground.

'It was a pity,' says Gerard Gili. 'Cantona was just beginning to make his mark at Marseille.' It had taken him a little while because even though Marseille was his home town, the atmosphere in the club was very different from the family-like atmosphere he had known at Auxerre. Here, the public pressure was one hundred times greater and he was playing in a team of big names and personalities. There is no doubt that as a player, he had an extraordinary talent. His technical qualities were first-rate but above all, his vision, his awareness of what was happening around him were way above average. Also his physical presence as a second striker, a number 10, was a great asset. He was extremely strong and he arrived at the club with this amazing confidence in his abilities. His mental strength was really something.

'People on the outside often portray him as an arrogant person but in everyday life, I found him to be a very humble guy, who worked very hard in training. He actually settled into the team quite well and was especially close with the younger players. I never had a problem with him as he accepted what I said to him without argument. I don't think that Eric has a problem with authority as long as there is respect on both sides, which means he has to think that the person standing in front of him is credible and worth listening to. I am not surprised by the success he found at Leeds and Manchester United, because his talent was there from the start. But I must admit that I was astonished by the extraordinary scale of his influence and popularity at Old Trafford.'

During the winter of 1989, the news that Cantona was leaving Marseille for Bordeaux on loan caused a sensation. The rivalry between the two dominant French clubs of the day was intense and the relationship between their two presidents, Tapie and Claude Bez, was one of open hatred and calumny. No one could understand why Tapie was prepared to hand over one of the most talented players in French football to his implacable enemy. Tapie gave little away in public but, speaking off the record to journalist Christian Jaurena, then at *Libération* newspaper, he revealed – in extremely vulgar and graphic terms – that he let Cantona go because he thought he would be sending a Trojan horse into his rival's camp. Or in Juarena's own words: 'Tapie said to me "Lending Cantona to Bordeaux is like being HIV positive and screwing Claude Bez up the arse without condoms."' Enchanté, Bernard.

Cantona, still only twenty-three, was soon on the move again, first to Montpellier and then to Nimes after a brief return to Marseille. Despite his temper, he was respected and liked by most of the players and coaches he worked with. 'Eric Cantona was absolutely not a problem,' says former French international Michel Mézy, his manager at Montpellier. 'At Montpellier, we had a few little difficulties at the beginning but he soon became a model team-mate and a great leader,' says Mézy. 'At first he was shy and introverted, but he liked to study the behaviour of his team-mates before opening himself up. Everybody has the image of Eric as being laidback person who didn't like to train. But it was quite the opposite. He was very industrious in his training. Eric is a perfectionist.

'What is true is that we often had to do a lot of talking because he always wanted everything to be explained and justified. And there was always that lingering feeling of injustice that could make him flare up in an instant. He was subject to terrible outbursts of anger.'

Cantona quickly established himself as a favourite amongst the Montpellier fans after being farmed out on another loan spell by Marseille, who continued to hold his registration. Montepellier president Louis Nicollin had also just bought Stéphane Paille, Cantona's best friend, from Sochaux and the fans were savouring the prospect of seeing an attacking combination that had played a major part in helping France win the European under-21 championship. But their dreams were short-lived. After just a few weeks Paille admitted that he couldn't settle at his new club, while Cantona threw one of his most remarkable tantrums in the changing room after a bad defeat at Lille. Cantona heard two of his team-mates, Michel Bernardet and Jean-Claude Lemoult, moaning about the game and mistakenly thought that they were criticizing him. He went berserk and attacked Lemoult with a football boot, hitting the little midfielder on the head over and over again in a wild frenzy, while screaming insults. His team-mates and some of the back-up staff eventually managed to pull him away. It seemed that Cantona had gone too far. 'You will never wear the Montpellier jersey again,' Nicollin told him.

Louis Nicollin is a huge figure in French football in every sense. Weighing an immense 300 pounds, he has the physical frame to match a giant personality. The man who made his fortune in collecting rubbish in the streets of France's southern cities has been called the Falstaff of French football: cunning, theatrical and always ready with a witty quip and a stream of 'bon mots'. His football club is his great passion, but the King of Montpellier, as he is also known, found his authority threatened by a revolt among his subjects who rose up in support of the Young Pretender Cantona after Nicollin disciplined him. When the Montpellier fans heard about Cantona's ban, they descended on the club and demanded his re-instatement. Sitting in the stands during one match, Nicollin was booed for the first time in his life and some fans even called for his resignation.

It was a difficult situation for Nicollin, because Cantona had refused to apologize publicly for the attack on his team-mate. 'It was the only time that Loulou, as we called him, ever found himself tottering on his throne,' recalls Eric Champel, who was working for the local news-paper, *Le Midi Libre*, at that time. 'So Nicollin swallowed his pride and he secretly met Cantona one evening in the car park of a local super-market where they apologized to each other and Cantona was restored to the team.'

Paille had been sold to Bordeaux, but Cantona thrived and today Nicollin has nothing but fond memories of the man he tried to sack. 'The team started to play well and Eric soon made his mark,' beams

Nicollin. 'We played some nice, attacking football and we won the French Cup. So I have good memories of Eric. Of course, everybody mentions that incident with Lemoult, but after it was resolved every-thing went well.'

Nicollin, a passionate Anglophobe, said he was delighted to see his former player winning over the English. 'I was really happy about Eric's success,' he says. 'When he was at Manchester United, it gave me a hard-on. I don't like the English and for a Frenchman to make them sing "La Marseillaise" is really something special. I think that the French government should have awarded him La Légion d'honneur.'

Cantona spent just one season at Montpellier, and was forced to return to Marseille as Nicollin didn't have enough money to buy his contract. His second spell in his home city was just as unsuccessful as his first. 'Dirty' Tapie, as he came to be known in France, was still the club's president and neither he nor Cantona were inclined to bury their differences. In the summer of 1991, he was packed off to Nimes where Michel Mézy – his coach at Montepellier – was now coach, and where he would be reunited with his friend Laurent Blanc, a future captain of France.

Despite the presence in the side of the two French internationals, Nimes struggled in the first half of the season and the frustration of play-ing in a losing side was clearly getting to Cantona. In a match against Saint-Etienne in December 1991, Cantona, increasingly incensed by the referee's decisions, protested so much that he was shown first a yellow card and then a red. Cantona reacted furiously, picking up the ball and launching it at the referee. The incident was to mark the end of Cantona's career in French club football. As he walked off the pitch, the headlines were already being written in the nation's newspapers, but what the journalists didn't know was what was happening in the tunnel after the match. Cantona laid in wait for Saint-Etienne defender Sylvain Kastendeuch, whom he held responsible for his sending off, and as the players trooped off he attacked him, first with a volley of abuse and then with a powerful punch to the face.

Cantona had written the journalists' story for them by his delinquent assault on the referee, but amazingly he felt they made too much of the incident. 'All I had written,' recalls Eric Champel, 'was that he was facing the prospect of a long suspension, but the next day he was on the telephone threatening to beat me up. He said to me "You little mother-f**ker, come to the club car park. I'll be waiting for you."'

Cantona was suspended. He didn't help his cause by telling the disciplinary committee that they were 'idiots'. The volatile star had had enough of French football and announced his retirement from the game at the age of twenty-five. Thankfully for Leeds and Manchester United, Michel Platini and Gérard Houllier (then, respectively, the retiring national coach and his successor) persuaded him to reconsider his decision and think about re-launching his career in England. 'Eric is an island' is how Houllier describes Cantona. So where better to send him than to that perfidious island nation across La Manche?

How strange that this man whose outrageous behaviour and temper tantrums made him a virtual 'untouchable' in his home country should find such glory and adoration in little England, with all its Francophobia and suspicion of foreigners. It was difficult to imagine the more puritan authorities in England putting up with that level of recklessness for more than a season or two. But it was in England that Cantona would feel most at home, and by the time he retired from football altogether he would say that he felt 'more English than French'. In France, he was considered a spoiled brat who was wasting his talent, but in England he achieved superstardom and a level of public adoration that left his compatriots across the Channel gasping in astonishment.

'In France, Eric had reached a dead end,' says Mézy. 'It really was time for him to leave France, but I was not surprised by his success in England. which was the perfect place for him as he had the time and the space to create on the pitch. I am not sure that he would have been as successful in Italy, where the football is slower and the defences tighter, or even in Spain. But in England, he was able to demonstrate the full range of his qualities.'

Cantona was given the chance to revive his career at Sheffield Wednesday, but after impressing manager Trevor Francis in a five-a-side game he refused Francis's polite request to stay on so he could prove himself on grass. Another affront to Cantona's egg-shell pride for which Leeds and Manchester United fans would be eternally grateful (although Leeds fans would quickly qualify their admiration for the Frenchman after his abrupt departure to their rivals from across the Pennines).

Cantona joined Howard Wilkinson's Leeds for the second half of the season and was an instant hit with the Elland Road crowd, despite playing well only in fits and starts. Gordon Strachan, the team captain, admits he found it impossible to fathom the workings of the Frenchman's mind. Part of the problem was that Cantona barely spoke any English, but for Strachan he was just plain weird. 'He was an enigma,' recalls Strachan. 'I knew him for almost a year and I could never get inside his mind. You'd need a more qualified person than me to work it out.'

Strachan, though, saw that Cantona possessed outstanding natural ability, although he felt that the Frenchman occasionally went missing in games and made little effort to adapt his style if the game didn't suit him. 'The sign of a great player is if he can do simple things well and he does them brilliantly,' he said. 'If there's nothing on, he lays the ball off and always to feet.'

In only their second season back in the top flight Leeds won the league championship for the first time in twenty-six years. By then, Cantona had established a strong rapport amongst the fans despite only being a peripheral figure. 'Ooh aah Cantona, say ooh aah Cantona,' shouted the crowd in the city centre as the team paraded the trophy. It seemed that Cantona had found a new home, a new football family prepared to embrace him despite his eccentricities. But six months after joining the Yorkshire club he was sitting in a function suite at Old Trafford in front of the nation's media being unveiled as a Manchester United player. Quite a slap in the face if you were a Leeds fan.

The reasons behind Cantona's sudden, unexpected move remain a bit of mystery and at the time wild rumours flew around Elland Road as the fans tried to make sense of his decision. Once the dust had settled, the general consensus was that Cantona simply didn't enjoy playing alongside Lee Chapman, a powerful and worthy centre-forward, but blessed with just a fraction of the Frenchman's talent. Whatever the reason for his departure in November 1993, at £1.2 million United manager Alex Ferguson had pulled off what turned out to be one of the best transfer deals in the history of English football.

If Cantona's cameo role had earned him cult status at Leeds, his impact on Manchester United was nothing short of miraculous. United had spent millions and millions of pounds buying players and restructuring their youth teams in an increasingly desperate pursuit of the league title they hadn't won for twenty-six years. Cantona provided the missing ingredient. United began to play like a team rather than a collection of expensive individuals as the Frenchman began to work his magic. Cantona didn't just score goals and set them up, he also linked play beautifully with the simplicity of his passing and the range of his vision. But perhaps the most important contribution he made to the United cause was in restoring the sense of arrogant swagger that had characterized the team in the days of Best, Law and Charlton at the end of the 1960s. When Cantona stood in the goalmouth with his hands on his hips, his chest puffed out, his nose in the air and his collars turned up, staring down the opposition fans like a Roman emperor surveying an unruly mob, he gave the club a sense of self-assurance and providence that had been missing for over a quarter of a century.

His five years at Old Trafford were the club's most successful in their history up until then. They won four league titles and two FA Cups – including the Double in 1996 under Cantona's captaincy – and they began to re-emerge as a team to be taken seriously in Europe. In 2001 he was voted the greatest Manchester United player of all time by a generation of fans most of whom never saw George Best weave his magic and almost certainly never saw Billy Meredith, the Welsh Wizard, in his prime between 1907 and 1921. Most dispassionate observers who had seen United talents come and go since the Second World War would go no further than to say that Cantona was one of the club's very best players. But what is certainly true is that no other player has had such a dynamic, galvanizing effect on the team. A football team is all about the chemistry of its players and Cantona was the missing ingredient needed for the explosive compound that United had been threatening to become for so many years. Cantona, for want of a better expression, was the missing link.

Cantona's time with United was the happiest period of his career, but controversy continued to stalk him season after season. In United manager Alex Ferguson, Cantona came across a figure with a fiery temper and will to win almost as powerful as his own. The Scotsman was a strict man who commanded instant and absolute respect among his players, just as Guy Roux had done at Auxerre. He was Cantona's kind of manager, a strong man who was prepared to indulge occasional outbursts so long as the player produced for him on the pitch and on the training ground. Other managers might not have been so tolerant of Cantona's indiscretions, but Ferguson not only understood the value of the Frenchman to his team on match day, but also saw the inspirational effect he was having on the emerging crop of youngsters like David Beckham, Paul Scholes and Ryan Giggs. For all his brushes with authority, Cantona was the most dedicated trainer in the United squad, a man who would put in hours of extra practice in order to work on particular areas of his game. He was not a football troublemaker in the English tradition of boozing and fighting – the only trouble Eric caused was on the pitch.

The Selhurst Park spectacular was certainly the high point – or low point, depending on how you view these incidents – of Cantona's remarkable career in England, but it was by no means his only walk on the wild side. When the Frenchman with the heavy Marseillaise twang finally mastered some basic English, he showed that he was perfectly happy to call a bent referee 'a bent referee' when he came across one. That's exactly what he did when United were eliminated from the Champions League after a defeat by Turkish side Galatasaray in Istanbul in 1995. 'It is obvious that some referees have been bought in this competition,' he was quoted as saying in French sports daily *L'Equipe*. 'And I ask myself whether Kurt Roethlisberger has been bought too.' (Roethlisberger, incidentally, was later banned when he was found guilty of trying to influence a Champions League match between Auxerre and Grasshopper Zurich the following season.)

It was against Galatasaray, too, that Cantona suffered his most spectacular loss of self-control on the European stage. The Ali Sam Yen stadium, known affectionately to Galatasaray fans as Hell, is one of the most intimidating grounds in world soccer, but Cantona gave the impression he thought he was at the Henley-on-Thames Crown Green Bowls Club, such was his lack of fear of the locals. In an incredible fit of pique, remarkable even by his own standards, the Frenchman booted the ball into some Galatasaray officials at the side of the pitch, insulted the referee, jostled with police, threw something into the increasingly volatile crowd and generally strutted about as if he was perfectly prepared to offer the whole crowd out and give half of Istanbul a good pasting in the club car park.

Cantona's departure from Old Trafford was every bit as unexpected and dramatic as his arrival five years earlier. At the end of the 1997 season, aged just thirty and at the peak of his powers, he announced his retirement from professional football – and this time it was for real. United fans were shocked, not least because they didn't have the chance to give him a rousing send-off at Old Trafford. The timing of his announcement, on the day of Chelsea's FA Cup win over Middlesborough, was curious. Some saw it as another act of eccentricity – even perversity if you were a Chelsea fan who felt he was stealing the club's thunder on their big day out at Wembley – but others saw it as a reflection of his humility, shunning the limelight and an orgy of tears and back-slapping at Old Trafford in order to slip quietly away whence he came.

• • •

Of course, Cantona's life didn't stop the moment he hung up his boots, and the Gallic firecracker continued to sparkle in his own peculiar way. It was perhaps fitting that the man at the centre of so many dramas should choose acting as his second career. There were predictable guffaws when he announced his next move shortly after his retirement from football. Cantona, however, was serious. Our first chance to admire his thespian skills came after he landed the role of the French ambassador in the highly acclaimed film *Elizabeth*, starring Cate Blanchett, Geoffrey Rush and Joseph Fiennes. His performance, in a small role, was considered by most critics to be satisfactory, although many football fans reported a strange dizziness and buzzing noise in their head when they saw the former United forward wandering around the big screen wearing tight velvet hosiery and a feathered hat.

Cantona has combined his acting career with a day job as the travelling sales representative for the promotion of the European Pro Beach Soccer League. He returned to England, to Richmond-upon-Thames and Hyde Park, to prove to a suspicious public that you didn't necessarily need a real beach or an exotic coastal setting to play the game. It was while he was in the capital that he announced, in heavily accented English, that he was in fact an Englishman and not a Frenchman after all. 'The bottom line is, I am English. I feel closer to England than France. I love the football here, the fans are very passionate,' he told reporters.

Nor has a new life on the beach – or a London sandpit – calmed the fire of indignation in his belly. 'I piss on the lot of you,' he announced to a panel of dumbfounded journalists on a live television show in France. Cantona had shown in the past that he was nothing if not a man of his word and the studio guests were taking no chances. They abruptly removed their microphones and walked off the set with fifteen minutes of the scheduled programme left to run, leaving Eric and the anchorman to spend some quality broadcast time together. Later, Patrick Urbini, a journalist with *L'Equipe*, admitted that he and his fellow guests were frightened by the rumbling of the Cantona volcano. 'We were genuinely scared,' said Urbini. 'We felt he was building up to something and then it all came out. He completely lost his rag and we left before he could punch us.'

Earlier on the show, in a rare instance of a public figure – and a footballer no less – singing the praises of English sports journalists, Cantona launched into an outburst about the quality of the French press: 'Six months after my moment of madness [his kung-fu kick at Selhurst Park], the English press voted me the best player in England. But the French press who had called me "indefensible" chose not to mention that. As far as I'm concerned "indefensible" is the worst insult. It's an adjective I would only use only for criminals.' One glance at his face confirmed that right then probably wasn't the best time to point out that Eric was in fact a man with a criminal record. But discretion, the French journalists seemed to think, was definitely the better part of valour.

Whether French journalists like it or not, Cantona will go down as one of the greats of modern English football, and will be forever worshipped at Manchester United as the player who launched them into the most successful period in their history.

FRANK McAVENNIE

A WEE BIT OF BOTHER

Rarely has an international footballer crashed from grace as spectacularly and painfully as Frank McAvennie. In the first half of his career, the Scotsman lived out the dreams of working-class boys up and down the country. One of the best footballers in the land, McAvennie won public adoration and earned huge sums of money; he dated Page Three girls, drank champagne and mingled with celebrities. The toughest choices facing him at the end of each day were: what vintage champagne will it be tonight and which of these girls do I go home with? His gift for putting footballs into the back of nets had launched him into a world of riches and glamour that would have been unthinkable when he was cleaning the roads in Glasgow just a few years earlier. McAvennie reached the peak of his game in the latter half of the 1980s, but within ten years his life was in freefall. Leaving behind him a trail of broken relationships, debts, court appearances, empty

bottles and cocaine wraps, McAvennie slid out of the bright lig
into the gloom of a far shadier world.

Many footballers become depressed when their playing days are
over. They no longer hear the spine-tingling sound of 30,000 people
chanting their names, they miss the camaraderie of the changing
room, the post-match celebrations and the surge of adrenaline that
comes from intense physical exertion and fierce competition. The
instant recognition in the streets gradually disappears, autograph
hunters have bigger fish to fry, the earnings dry up and the search
for a new career begins. The only job most have known since they
were young teenagers is playing football, and most professionals
have no other qualifications to help them establish an alternative
career, and there are only limited amounts of coaching jobs and
media punditry positions to go around. Some prosper, but many
more lose out. Today, footballers earn phenomenally more than players from previous generations and they are also better managed and
better advised off the pitch. Some still go off the rails no matter how
much money they earn or how well they're advised, but far fewer
than in previous eras.

The prospect of building another career after a life as a football
star would be daunting anyhow, but for Frank McAvennie the future is
potentially bleak. His reputation undermined by his association with
drugs and his earnings long since banked by a thousand grateful bar
owners, this former West Ham and Celtic idol now lives in a flat in
Gateshead and faces a tough battle just to piece together some
semblance of a life in his grave new world.

•••

Frank McAvennie's career at the top of British football was too brief
for him to be considered one of the country's great players, but for two

seasons – one at West Ham and one at Celtic – he played as well as any striker in Europe. And for his performances at that time, he will be forever remembered as a hero by the followers of those clubs.

Born in Milton, Glasgow in 1959, McAvennie signed his first professional forms with St Mirren in 1980, the first of nine different clubs he would play for over sixteen years. He had been spotted by talent scouts, who had actually come to watch another player, but found themselves increasingly drawn by this unlikely figure. McAvennie was slightly built and didn't appear to have the physical attributes to make it at the highest grade – and a loathing for training did not help his reputation.

'I remember the first time I met Frank... it was pre-season training,' recalls his former St Mirren team-mate Ian McLeod. 'I walked into the dressing room and here was this young, skinny boy sitting in the corner. He was my partner up front for next season and I remember looking at him and saying: "I'll give you a couple of weeks." As it turned out, Frank was just a sensation that season.' McAvennie didn't make his league debut until the 1981/82 season, but he quickly made an impact, scoring twice in a 4-3 victory over Airdrie. By the end of the season he had been called into the Scotland Under-21 side and was voted Young Player of the Year.

Andy McInnes, a reporter who knew McAvennie well at St Mirren, remembers the skinny boy with the curly ginger hair as an easy-going, down-to-earth local lad. 'One year I invited him as my guest to the football writers' Player of the Year dinner in Scotland,' says McInnes. 'We were all sitting there in our bow ties and so on and I can remember the look on everyone's faces when Frank turned up wearing a leather jacket and a T-shirt. We were all drinking wine, but Frank was happy with his pints of heavy. That was what he was like in the early days.'

Scotland was rich in football talent in the early 1980s, but most of the best players inevitably found their way into the more lucrative world of English football. McAvennie's first suitors from south of the border were Luton Town, then holding their own in the old First Division. His agent Bill McMurdo took McAvennie to a meeting with manager David Pleat and the club's uncompromising chairman David Evans, a Conservative MP and one of Margaret Thatcher's personal favourites. The talks did not go well. In fact, they ended deep into the night with Evans telling McAvennie and McMurdo to 'F**k off back to Scotland'. But all was not lost. As they left the meeting, McMurdo woke up West Ham manager John Lyall. They met in a motorway service station at four o'clock in the morning, where a deal was quickly struck.

McAvennie was barely known south of the border when he arrived at West Ham in 1985, but by the end of his first season he had established himself as one of the leading footballers in the country. He was bought as a midfielder but after an early injury to Paul Goddard, he was asked to play up front – with astonishing consequences. McAvennie put away twenty-six goals in 1985/86 in a lethal partnership with Tony Cottee who scored twenty as West Ham finished third in the league, their highest ever position. McAvennie, a stranger to the wider football world nine months earlier, came within a goal of winning Europe's Golden Boot award for the most prolific striker, but was beaten to the prize by Everton's Gary Lineker on the last day of the season.

Leslie Grantham, the actor best known for his part as Dirty Den in *EastEnders*, is a West Ham regular who remembers with glee McAvennie's remarkable impact on the East London club. 'Frank was just phenomenal,' Grantham recalls. 'Not only did he make goals and score them, he would often start the move that four or five passes later would end up with him bashing it in the back of the net. He was the beacon that we were looking for. I think everyone felt that the good times were about to come again.'

Charlie Nicholas, another Scottish striker with a love of the nightlife (inevitably dubbed 'Champagne Charlie' by the newspapers), was a better-known and more experienced player than his compatriot, but he was struggling to make an impact at Arsenal when McAvennie burst on to the scene. 'He was so skinny it was unbelievable,' remembers Nicholas. 'I never thought he would ever make it big in football. I was surprised how quickly he adapted to England, because it was taking me time. But Frank just came and blew them away.'

McAvennie struck up an almost instant rapport with the West Ham crowd – and it wasn't just his goals they appreciated. McAvennie would run himself into the ground for his team-mates, chasing balls other strikers would have given up as lost causes and when he scored, he looked like he was about to burst with joy. 'The one enduring memory I have of Frank McAvennie was the smile from ear to ear when he scored,' says Ken Dyer, a reporter with London's *Evening Standard* who covered many of West Ham's matches during this period. 'He had that look of sheer, undiluted pleasure on his face as if it was... the best thing in the world. The fans took to him because of that. He played as though he was really enjoying his work. He was a cult figure for them, just as Paolo Di Canio is today. They just loved him.'

McAvennie's success on the pitch was matched by his flair in the capital's leading nightclubs. A television strike meant that football was off the nation's screens for much of the season, allowing the young West Ham player to hit the West End without fear of being noticed. But by the end of the season McAvennie was a household name and face as the tabloids jumped on this publicity-hungry, good-looking athlete who had swapped his natural ginger curls for a peroxide blond

New Romantic image. Rampant hooliganism had lowered the image of English football to new depths at home as well as abroad, and apart from the sports reporters the rest of the media took little interest in the off-pitch antics of the country's footballers. But McAvennie's glamorous lifestyle would play a small part in restoring some of the superficial gloss to the game and he was soon appearing in the front pages of the tabloids, more often than not pictured going in or out of Stringfellows with a blonde on his arm. With money coming in from advertising and media contacts, McAvennie was soon earning over £5,000 a week, a considerable sum of money at the time.

It was McAvennie's appearance on *Wogan*, the BBC chat show, that lifted him to a new level of celebrity. 'There was some sort of camera strike on and nobody really knew what the top scorer in England looked like until he went on the *Wogan* show,' recalls *Sun* reporter Matt Bandoris. 'The next day when he went out to meet his mum at Heathrow airport he was mobbed. He couldn't move. From that moment on, every temptation came his way: Page Three girls, drugs. It was all put on a plate for him. Today he jokes that it was Terry Wogan who put him on the rocky road to ruin.'

Striker John Fashanu, a member of Wimbledon's abrasive 'Crazy Gang' side of the late 1980s, said McAvennie's playful, casual nature made him doubly dangerous, as opponents could be lulled into ignoring his potential threat. 'Frankie Mac was always very, very friendly on the pitch,' says Fashanu. 'He was one of these players who would have a banter with you over ninety minutes. Whether you were winning 1-0 or you were losing 2-0 you could always rely on Frankie for a joke.

'But as a player he reminded me of Gary Lineker. He'd be doing absolutely nothing, all game, then all of a sudden he'd produce a couple of flashes of genius and he'd got two goals. We didn't know anything about him at all before he arrived in England. Then suddenly he was there, an established part of the scene, larger than life.'

McAvennie's fellow Scot and West Ham team-mate Ray Stewart believes that all the publicity about his lifestyle has buried the fact that he was one of the most committed and energetic players of his day, who would run the socks off defenders all match. 'What people used to notice about Frank was that he was a hard-working player,' says Stewart. 'Certainly, for me he was tremendous because he'd make my bad passes look like very good ones, as he would chase them seventy yards and let people know he'd been there.'

After that spellbinding first season, McAvennie looked set to become a major feature of English soccer for years to come. His agent Bill McMurdo believes that his girlfriend of the time played a major role in keeping the lid on his nightlife. 'When he first moved down there, I would say that for the first year he was as good as gold,' says McMurdo. 'He concentrated on the football. He was very seldom out without Anita, his fiancée at that time. For my money, she was the best person for him because, to a degree, she could control him. She was a great disciplinarian and he got away with nothing. When he finished with her I felt that he went to the wall.'

When McAvennie wasn't in a permanent relationship, he played the field. 'Frank always had women eating out of his hands,' says McMurdo, who has also represented George Best and Maurice 'Mo' Johnston amongst others. 'Old women, young women, middle-aged women – there was just something about him that they took to. You may find this hard to believe, but most of the time he was pretty loyal to whomever he was with. The times he started seeing a lot of women was when there was nobody there.'

McAvennie liked getting engaged, but was not so keen on the marriage part of the arrangement. 'He's had more engagements than the Queen's got soldiers,' quips McMurdo. One fiancée McAvennie did marry was Laura – the mother of his son Jake – whom he lived with for five years after his playing career came to an end. 'Frank tells a funny story against himself about when they got married and they went into the vestry to sign the register and I was sent for by the priest who tells me they have a problem: they can't agree on the marriage contract. Laura wants it for life and Frank wants it for three years with a three-year option.'

McAvennie's highest-profile relationship in the late 1980s was with Page Three girl Jenny Blyth. At first the glamorous young lovers seemed made for each other, but their extravagant lifestyle would soon cost them their friendship and much of their livelihood. The relationship would end in bitter acrimony as McAvennie set up home with another woman, leaving Jenny distraught at her treatment. Years later McAvennie sold an unflattering story to one of the tabloids about their time together, which Jenny says hurt her more than anything else in their stormy relationship.

McMurdo maintains it was Jenny, not Frank, who had the taste for the champagne. 'I'll always remember her saying to me, "When you take a sip of this pink champagne it's like an angel having an orgasm on the tip of your tongue." Frank had this image that he always drank champagne, but I thought that was a bit of a myth in some ways because he was really a lager man. He liked lager quite a bit as well as a wee vodka.'

Blyth, who is no longer in contact with her former fiancé, regrets that their relationship ended in such bitter warfare, with the truth of what happened one of the first casualties. 'We met at Stringfellows for

Maria Whittaker's eighteenth birthday party but I wasn't particularly attracted to Frank at all for quite some time,' she recalls. 'Eventually we became the sort of poor man's Posh and Becks of the time, I suppose, but not nearly on the same scale. We had the typical footballer/Page Three girl mock-Tudor mansion in Essex. In the article that Frank did, which was a total character assassination of me, he tried to make out as if he'd lost all these hundreds of thousands of pounds because he went out with me. But I never expected to have a house like that at all. I was looking at much more modest houses.'

With the money rolling in, McAvennie left no cliché out as he launched himself into a heady rock-and-roll lifestyle. He even bought a number plate for his black Capri that read UP U2. 'He was enjoying the birds, he was enjoying the champagne and enjoying the lifestyle – and he had a few nice cars too,' says Ray Stewart. 'I remember when he got a beautiful Capri 2.8, it was stolen the very next day so Frank just bought another one. Nothing seemed to bother him.'

Peter Stringfellow believes that McAvennie in his glory days was responsible for restoring some of the lost glamour to football's image. 'When [Stringfellows] came to London in 1980, we weren't particularly keen on footballers,' he explains. 'They didn't have the money, it certainly wasn't glamorous and we didn't have the entourages we get today. To be honest, we weren't too keen on being associated with football because of the lager lout image. The press was totally disinterested in them as far as the [nightclub] scene went. But it slowly changed – and then along came Frank. You got the feeling when Frank walked in that he wanted to be a star. He looked and acted like a star and I liked that.

'Other football teams caused trouble but I never saw Frank bringing any. He just loved the glamorous life, which suited me fine. I'd sit with him, have a few glasses of champagne; I'd got my girls and he'd got his girls.'

• • •

McAvennie made his debut for Scotland in 1986 and he could have virtually picked himself for the squad for the 1986 World Cup finals in Mexico following his brilliant first season at West Ham. In all, he played five times for his country, but just as he wouldn't fulfil his potential at club level, he failed to make a significant impact at international level. There were flashes of excellence, but they were no more than that. His international team-mates remember him as much for his post-match performances as they do for his contributions on the pitch.

'I remember when, after Scotland played England at Wembley, myself and Mo Johnson let Frank take us out the night after the game,' recalls fellow striker Ally McCoist, McAvennie's rival at Rangers. 'Frank said, "We are going to take the Tube", and I wondered whether that was such a good idea. Sure enough, what seemed to be the entire crew of the Millwall Headhunters got into our carriage and there were Union Jacks everywhere, skinheads with braces. They all had tattoos on their teeth! I said to Frank that I was getting off at the next stop but the next minute he was playing cards with them. Frank had butted his way in and just made light of the whole situation and he even ended up taking money off them at Shoot Pontoon. It was absolutely brilliant.'

Sadly for McAvennie and West Ham fans, there would be no repeat of his stunning first season at the club. The extravagant lifestyle continued but as the goals and his general form dried up in the 1986/87 season, McAvennie began to think about moving clubs. Former Arsenal and Republic of Ireland midfielder Liam Brady joined West Ham in the latter part of the season as McAvennie's form began to slide. 'My first experience of Frank was when I came back from Italy. West Ham had had a brilliant season the year before, but the bubble had burst and they were struggling in the lower half of the First Division,' he remembers. 'Frank wanted away and I think there were a lot of clubs interested in him because he'd had such a good season in the First Division in the year before.'

Brady knew all about McAvennie's lifestyle and was taken aback when he saw how much effort the Glasgow bon viveur put into his match performances. 'It was funny in the dressing room because there was always something in the tabloid newspapers about Frank,' says Brady. 'But Frank was a 100 per cent trier. He would chase balls into the corner that a lot of centre forwards would not bother with. He would also tackle centre backs, chase them down and win balls he wasn't expected to win. The crowd loves anybody who gives that kind of effort and on top of that he could score goals. He was just a really infectious player, who had this rapport with the fans. They loved him and when he went it was a sad day for West Ham.' But Brady is pragmatic about McAvennie's departure from Upton Park: 'I know for a fact John Lyall didn't really want to lose him, but he obviously knew about Frank's lifestyle. Every manager does, because you get fans ringing them up saying: "I saw McAvennie out last night" or "I saw Gascoigne out last night."'

Ian McLeod, McAvennie's former St Mirren team-mate, was one of several old friends who found it difficult to fit into his new, ritzy way of life. It wasn't that McAvennie himself had changed, so much as that the world he moved in was so far removed from the one he had known a few years earlier. Whereas once McAvennie would go and have a few quiet beers in a run-of-the-mill pub with a group of his mates, now he would only be found in the smartest joints surrounded by a crowd of hangers-on pretending to be his friends and lapping up his carefree generosity. 'I found it difficult at times when we used to go out socializing,' McLeod admits. 'We'd have been out for no more than five or ten minutes together when Frank would get involved elsewhere and our night together was over. I got left on my own and people used to come up to me and say "Are you Frank McAvennie's pal?" and I would say, "No, I'm Ian McLeod."'

Journalist Andy McInnes couldn't believe the scale of the player's extravagance. 'When the team had got their win bonus, anything from nine hundred to fifteen hundred quid, Frank would use his as his credit for the night,' McInnes explains. 'He would just go into the nearest nightclub or restaurant and spend it all.'

But McAvennie was still capable of playing as hard on the pitch as he did off it. John Fashanu was stunned when he saw McAvennie in a London nightclub in the small hours of Saturday morning, less than twelve hours before the weekend programme kicked off. 'I wasn't playing because I was suspended and I went upstairs at Stringfellows where I saw a whole group of people drinking champagne and having a great time. I thought it was probably Rod Stewart's group or George Michael's but lo and behold, it was Frankie Mac. I went up to him just before I was leaving – it must have been around four-thirty, and I said: "Haven't you got a game tomorrow?" He said: "Yeah, that'll be right, Fash." When I woke up in the afternoon I turned on Teletext and Frank had got a hat-trick! The man's stamina must be incredible.'

• • •

McAvennie's form slumped in his second season at West Ham and when he was linked with a move to Celtic he decided to move on. The Upton Park club accepted there was little point in trying to hang on to him if his heart was not in playing for them. Leaving behind his favourite West End nightclubs, McAvennie fulfilled a lifelong ambition when he signed for Celtic for £750,000. 'In my view, Frank was the best Celtic signing in the last twenty-five years, with the exception of [Henrik] Larsson,' says McMurdo. 'I think he was one of the best talents, young talents, that we had in the Scottish game for years and years. He was a tremendous player, but I think he could have done even better.

'He'd always been linked with Celtic and to go there was his childhood dream. I genuinely believe that there's no other club he would have come back to Scotland for. Celtic paid him top dollar and broke their wage structure but I don't think it was the money, because he could have got the same amount in England, perhaps even more.'

McAvennie's first season at Celtic was every bit as sensational as his first at West Ham. He struck up a deadly partnership with Andy Walker just as he had with Tony Cottee two seasons earlier. He scored thirty-four goals in sixty-six games for the Bhoys, including two in the Scottish Cup Final against Dundee United to clinch the Double in the club's centenary year. 'Nobody will convince me otherwise, for me the '88 season when Celtic won the double was down to Frank,' says McMurdo.

The only low spot in the season was when McAvennie was sent off after a goalmouth scuffle in an extraordinarily combustible Old Firm encounter with Rangers at Ibrox in October. Rangers' goalkeeper Chris Woods and defender Terry Butcher were also dismissed and all three of them – together with Rangers' Graham Roberts – later appeared in court on breach of the peace charges. McAvennie was accused in court of causing the altercation, but he was acquitted while Butcher and Woods were both found guilty and fined. The case against Roberts was not proven.

If Celtic fans were hoping that McAvennie would continue his prolific scoring the following season, they were to be disappointed. Just as he had in his two years at West Ham, he blew very hot one season and very cold the next; it was never temperate in Frank McAvennie's world. The magnetic pull of London's West End was at the heart of his unrest and sudden loss of form. He began to divide his time between the two cities, flying back and forth throughout the week at great cost to his bank balance and even greater cost to his physical condition. The travelling was tiring and unsettling and McAvennie put further strain on himself by partying with his now customary gusto when he returned to London's all-night clubs. Celtic tried everything in their power to keep him, but were forced to accept that there was little point in paying a player enormous wages when his mind and body were elsewhere for much of the time.

McAvennie's career might have turned out very differently if Arsenal manager George Graham had had his way. Arsenal were top of the table and Graham matched West Ham's offer of £1.25 million, figuring the Scotsman would rather play for a successful team than one struggling in the relegation zone. But he was to be disappointed. McAvennie opted for the club that had helped launch his career, where he still had a host of good friends and memories.

He returned to West Ham in March 1989, but any excitement over the reunion was short-lived. Bringing back McAvennie was a final desperate measure by a side battling relegation and changing room unrest. Hopes had soared amongst Hammers fans that McAvennie would have a similar impact on the team to the one he had when he arrived as a virtual unknown just a few years earlier. But, playing in an unhappy team lacking confidence and cohesion in equal measure, he failed to save them.

'I suppose Frank was part of the disco set,' says Leslie Grantham. 'George Best always seemed to attract Miss Worlds; Frank seemed to attract the Page Three girls, and I think Frank was scoring as much off the field as he was on it. Unfortunately, if you're a West Ham supporter and you're fighting relegation, you're not interested in how many times he scores a week in his bed, you want to know how many times he'll score in the back of the net.'

Liam Brady, who would retire from the game that year, recalls the miserable atmosphere in the dressing room as West Ham slid inexorably towards the Second Division. 'A lot of the players wanted to leave, including Tony Cottee and Paul Ince,' Brady explains. 'We were struggling and John Lyall needed to find someone who was going to turn things round and as far as the fans were concerned, there was only one man and that was Frank McAvennie. But it didn't quite work. He wasn't really looking after himself and I don't think he was the same player he was when he came first time round.'

Worse was to follow in the first game of the new season, when McAvennie shattered his leg in a collision with Stoke's Chris Kamara. It was a terrible break that kept him on the sidelines for a year and effectively ended his career as a serious footballer. McAvennie would return for a few more seasons, playing for a variety of clubs in England and Scotland, but it was clear that he was a spent force. During his long spell on the sidelines, McAvennie had every day and every night and every opportunity to enjoy himself in the only way he knew how – by going out and partying. Managers always fear for their players when they suffer a bad injury, as the temptation to drown their sorrows often proves to be irresistible. For a player like McAvennie, with a love of the high life, the threat to his career was less the injury itself than what he might do to his body and soul while he recuperated.

McAvennie says he first tried cocaine during this long lay-off when he was drunk in a bar. 'Why not? One line won't harm,' he thought. His friends believe that this period was the true beginning of the end for the Scotland striker, the start of a slow and painful slide into broken relationships, money problems, drugs and court cases.

'I think the injury had a lot to do with it, because he had a lot of time on his hands,' reflects McMurdo. 'He had even more time to socialize. I was aware that in some of the clubs that he was going to about 90 per cent of the celebrities and footballers who were going there were taking drugs. I suppose I deluded myself that Frank wouldn't. I think I could have been a wee bit more vigilant in some ways.'

Money was also starting to be a problem. McAvennie continued to spend recklessly, not just on himself but also on the so-called friends he associated with. 'There were a lot of hangers-on,' admits McMurdo. 'Frank is one of the most generous guys you would ever come across. Every time I was in his company, particularly in London, he seemed to be the only one that was finding any money. Now you could imagine that happening if you're with guys who don't have any money, but these people were supposed to be successful businessmen.

'I also felt that trying to keep two houses going at the one time was a tremendous drain on his financial resources,' he adds, 'and I don't think he's ever recovered from that. Frank would agree that if he had looked after his money properly, he probably would never have needed to work again.'

• • •

It says something for the qualities of McAvennie as a player and a character that both West Ham and Celtic were prepared to welcome him back for second spells – and pay good money to get him and high wages to keep him happy. But it also says something about the culture of British football at the time. Today, most leading footballers with a taste for the booze try to maintain some kind of discretion on their nights out, but in McAvennie's time, no one, not even managers, seemed particularly concerned about players drinking heavily. Only in recent years, with the arrival of more health-conscious foreigners as well as the confessions of various addictions by high-profile players such as Tony Adams, Paul Merson and Paul Gascoigne, has heavy drinking among players been widely condemned.

But Celtic were perfectly happy to re-employ a player whose raucous lifestyle could be read about in the national newspapers on a near-weekly basis. Sad to say, McAvennie gave little return on the club's investment in him. 'Frank scored a few goals and I suppose he did OK,' says Brady, who managed Celtic between 1991 and 1993. 'But it was obviously going to be short term with Frank, because his lifestyle just didn't lend itself to getting on with the manager. A manager tries to have discipline in the club, but Frank really wasn't interested in that.

'He just wouldn't listen. If you could have had a bet on who was going to get into trouble, or who was going to end up skint after a playing career [from which they] really should have earned quite a lot of money, Frank would be my number one candidate, I'm afraid to say. If he got a break somewhere now, maybe in television or something like that, he'd probably go and blow that, because that's the kind of guy he is.'

Harsh words indeed, but the facts back them up. Part of the problem was that McAvennie was unable to shake off his love of London and its glamorous nightclubs. With drugs now an established part of the club scene, the temptations that surrounded him proved to be too strong. In 1994, he admitted his cocaine use.

'He just kept being Jack the Lad, burying his head in the sand and buying the world and their wife a bottle of champagne,' says Jenny Blyth, whose relationship with McAvennie began to deteriorate in tandem with his decline as a player. His old friend Ian McLeod says he had no idea that drugs had become such a feature of McAvennie's life. 'I never knew Frank was taking drugs at all,' he confesses. 'I think Frank got caught up with different people wanting to get into his company, maybe not the right type of people. Frank just got led down that road.'

Ray Stewart, his former West Ham team-mate, says that McAvennie's problems arose out of his generosity and his trusting and carefree nature. He simply couldn't say 'no' to anyone. 'I was always very much aware that certain people needed to be kept at arm's length, and you'd introduce Frank to them and Frank would say, "Oh aye, we need to watch them and keep them at arm's length." But before you knew where you were, he'd be standing at the bar having a good crack with them.'

'But there is a side to Frank that no one ever talks about or writes about,' Stewart insists, 'and that's all the charity work he did. Whenever I asked him to help out he would be right there saying, "What do you need? What do you want me to do?" I think that's the good side of Frank McAvennie that people don't really look at, providing children with respirator machines and so on. People don't look at that on the media side, they always look at the booze and the birds with Frank. But he had a very, very soft side to him.' Indeed, as far as Stewart is concerned, this was Frank McAvennie's fatal flaw: 'He was always trying to give everybody his time and that was probably his downfall. He was too nice to everybody.'

The public first became aware of McAvennie's association with drugs when he was arrested at Glasgow airport after cocaine was found in his wallet. ('It's just a wee bit of charlie,' he famously told officials.) He was convicted of possession, but was involved in a far more serious court case in 1996 when he and some of his associates were arrested at Dover docks as Customs officers seized £200,000 in cash from their car. Magistrates in Dover were satisfied that the cash, half of it McAvennie's, was to pay for drugs in Holland to be smuggled into England. McAvennie gave various different accounts of where the money was going, claiming that the money was swindled out of him and that he thought it was going towards buying a boat for a deep-sea treasure hunt. He blamed his lawyers and said the only reason he didn't appeal against the court's decision was because his mother had had a heart attack brought on by the tension of seeing her son on trial. He also raised an eyebrow in court by claiming not to know his alleged co-conspirator, only to describe him as a 'nice guy' moments later.

'The story was that he was investing £100,000 into a sunken treasure ship,' says McMurdo. 'He said after the event that the reason he never told me was because I would not have allowed it to happen. I said: "Well that's true, because if you're going to invest that sort of money, I would have wanted you to do it contractually. I'd have wanted the cheque to go into the bank and have some guarantees." He shouldn't have been involved. I had to go down to Dover to give evidence and I had words with him, as you can imagine.'

Ally McCoist finds it difficult not to see the funny side of McAvennie's defence. 'I just thought it was magic. I just had this vision of Frank sailing across the channel like Blackbeard the Pirate and this big mast with a skull and crossbones on it, looking for a treasure chest. It could only be Frank, couldn't it? I just thought it was hilarious. Oh! Frankie boy!'

Matt Bandoris of *The Sun* says McAvennie is innocent enough to have really thought that the money was actually going towards a sunken treasure venture. 'I think he genuinely believed there was a shipwreck with ancient Greek pottery on it that was going to make him a fortune,' says Bandoris. 'Would anyone in their right minds ever send £100,000 in a suitcase over to Amsterdam? You'd automatically think it's a drug deal. But Frank will bore the ears off you talking about this shipwreck, so much so that even the people in his pub used to call him "Captain" and buy him stuffed parrots. He really believed that that was going to be his big pay day. He's always got a scheme on the go, always believes there's just something around the corner.

'I like Frank but I think he's stunningly naive. I think he knows several dodgy characters that are always trying to sell him get-rich-quick schemes. But he's never going to be a criminal mastermind because I don't think he's intelligent enough... He doesn't intend to get into trouble, but he will always end up either broke or in jail.'

● ● ●

McAvennie has found more stability in his life since meeting Karen Lamberti, his latest love. ('I'd never heard of him in my life,' says Karen, who works in a restaurant in Newcastle, 'I've never been into football.') But towards the end of 2000, their relationship had to weather the worst ordeal so far in Frank McAvennie's relentlessly tempestuous, controversy-ridden life, when he appeared in Newcastle Crown Court charged with conspiracy to supply £110,000 worth of Ecstasy tablets and amphetamines. Karen recalls with horror the moment she discovered her boyfriend had been arrested. 'I realized the police had been in and they'd been searching the house. He was denied bail and I was shocked. You just don't know what's going on. Obviously you're worried and the phone... never stopped ringing.'

McAvennie spent four weeks on remand in a Durham prison before his case was tried. The court heard how undercover national crime squad detectives saw him in a car with a friend and an acquaintance travelling to a house in Newcastle to pick up drugs. The acquaintance later took a train to Glasgow and was arrested with 5,000 Ecstasy tablets and 11lbs of amphetamine paste.

Charlie Nicholas says he was dumbfounded when he heard the news of McAvennie's arrest a few days after he had spoken to him on the telephone. McAvennie had told Nicholas he was settling down with the help of his new girlfriend and looking for a steady job in football. 'Coaching was a direction he wanted to look at,' says Nicholas. 'He's got a lot of friends in football who might have given him an opportunity in the youth teams or some sort of an academy. He sounded far more positive, but within four days it hit the newspapers that he was [implicated] in the drug scene again. I just thought, that's the end, he's disappointing everybody again, not just his friends, but his family. I was quite saddened when I read it. I thought he was probably going to have to serve his time. But maybe in the long term this will be something that he has to do to sort his head out.'

If convicted, the former football idol faced up to ten years in prison. McAvennie admitted he was in the car but insisted that he knew nothing about any drug deal. The jury acquitted him and McAvennie broke down in tears of relief as the verdict was read out. He always claimed the charges were ridiculous, and today he scoffs at the suggestion that he was a drug dealer. In an earlier court appearance he received a conditional discharge for possessing 40g of cocaine hidden in a cigarette packet. As he left court, he vowed: 'I will never touch drugs again and I urge any youngsters to do the same. Supplying drugs is wrong. I would never, ever sell drugs.'

After speaking to the press, McAvennie and his girlfriend headed for the nearest bar to celebrate his new lease of life. 'When he got not guilty, it was just the biggest relief in the world,' admits Karen. 'It was over and done with and you can start really planning your future again. Afterwards we phoned his mum and dad straightaway and then went straight to the pub opposite. All the jury came in and shook his hand.'

McAvennie's friends hope that his brush with long-term imprisonment will act as a final wake-up call for the fun-loving rogue who just can't say 'no'. 'Not knowing the full ins and outs of the court case, all I can hope is that he's learned his lessons, because everybody really has a genuine affection for Frank,' says Ally McCoist. 'Nobody wants to see him in jail, that's the last place you want to see Frank McAvennie.'

With the exception of one or two old girlfriends, it's difficult to find anyone with a bad word to say about Frank McAvennie. By almost universal consensus, he is a loveable, naive Jack the Lad who can't help getting into scrapes. Leslie Grantham believes McAvennie provided a textbook case of the rags-to-riches story gone wrong. 'I think part of the reason for his downfall is the fact that Frank's your working-class boy who's made good,' he argues. 'If you're a kid that's not got any toys and you're locked in Hamley's overnight, you're going to go mad, aren't you? Footballers haven't always earned huge amounts of money, but Frank was coming into it at the time when they were making good cash... I don't think he's upset by what has happened to him. He's had a good time. He's still got his legs. He's not suffering from Alzheimer's. He's not in a wheelchair. As far as I'm concerned, he'll always be a star because he was a fantastic footballer and a lovely guy.

'I can't be judgmental,' Grantham continues. 'He just took some drugs, put something up his nose, and I'm sure he's not the only one and I'm sure he won't be the last. I think you have to be what you have to be. I think the minute you impose a strict regime on someone like Frank, you take away any individuality and any spark of brilliance that he has. My only bit of advice that I would like to have said to Frank at the time was, "Leave some women for someone else, mate. For God's sake, don't eat all the biscuits in the tin."'

Unsurprisingly, Jenny Blyth takes a less charitable view of her former lover. 'We were together just over five years and I suppose after about three he started to change. West Ham didn't want to renew his contract and nobody else was coming in for him at all, and he drank more and took more coke to try and hide from it.' Blyth says she wanted to sue McAvennie and the newspaper for which he wrote an article that she claims severely damaged her reputation, but she did not have the money to fight. 'There was a particular piece in the article saying that he spent thousands on my habit. I was just horrified because, although our relationship ended very acrimoniously, I still believed that deep down there was part of the old Frank that would have a bit of respect for our relationship. Since we've split up, I think everybody's seen the road he's gone down and he can't blame me for that now. He's just gone really off the rails...

'He used to come home at the weekends and he was fine and we had a normal sex life and he told me he loved me... And then one day he said that he was going to be going on a coaching course to give him something to do after his football career had finished. The next day, the *News of the World* rang me up and said: "What do you think about the fact Frank's gone off to the Bahamas with another girl?" I couldn't get hold of him for about six weeks after that. I just couldn't believe that after five years of living with someone, [he] couldn't have the decency to at least tell [me] straight what's going on. I just think I deserved a bit better than that after five years.'

You'd be wrong, however, to think that Frank McAvennie is blind to his faults and their repercussions. In a candid interview with the *Observer Monthly*, he spoke of the torment caused by his association with drugs, explaining the anguish he felt when his young son saw a picture of him in a drugs-related newspaper story and shouted: 'Look, it's my daddy!' He is determined to stay clear of drugs, but fears that his shady past will prevent him getting the coaching job he needs.

His girlfriend Karen believes McAvennie will always be stigmatized because he didn't go through a public catharsis. 'You get someone like Elton John, who was on TV the other night saying how he used to get it flown in by aeroplane, but now he's reformed so that's OK. Because he said, "Yes I had a problem", it's OK. Frank hasn't got a problem and because he's always said, "No, I don't have a problem," he's not getting the sympathy vote.'

His friends are keeping their fingers crossed that Frank McAvennie can stay on the straight and narrow. They say there's never been much point in trying to restrict McAvennie, because he would always wriggle free and return to the life he enjoyed. 'I don't know if you'd have got the brilliant Frank McAvennie *on* the park, if you curtailed him *off* it,' argues his former international team-mate McCoist. 'I think if you'd said, "Right Frank, you're in the house every night at eight o'clock, tucked into bed with a pot of tea", his head would have blown up.'

MARADONA

THE BAD BOY'S BAD BOY

Towards the end of 2001 the BBC asked the British people to vote for the greatest Briton of all time. Leading candidates included the statesman Winston Churchill, poet and playwright William Shakespeare, scientists Charles Darwin and Isaac Newton, Admiral Horatio Nelson, novelist Charles Dickens, Queen Victoria, musician John Lennon, Margaret Thatcher and the Victorian engineer Isambard Kingdom Brunel. Churchill, whose personality dominated British life for much of the first half of the twentieth century, won by a comfortable margin, with Shakespeare second and Nelson third. Famous footballers, including England captain David Beckham, barely registered in the vote.

If a similar survey was to be held in Argentina, the outright winner would be a convicted criminal and drug addict who has shot journalists with an air rifle, fathered a love child whom he refuses to acknowledge and who is wanted for questioning by the Italian tax authorities. He also happens to be one of the greatest footballers who has ever lived. Some people, mainly Argentinians, say Diego Armando Maradona was *the* greatest.

At 5'4", Maradona was tiny compared to the titanic athletes of modern football. But he was blessed with incredible balance, a low centre of gravity, quick feet, an even quicker mind, great vision, power and speed, demonic determination and a total belief in the superiority of his abilities. The boy from the suburbs of Buenos Aires became the most feared player to grace a football pitch since Pelé.

To look at him in the year 2001 after his admission to a rehabilitation clinic, it was uncomfortable to recall that this ill, bloated man was only recently delighting millions of people across the globe with the magic of his football. Despite his spectacular fall from grace, Maradona has never lost his cult status in Argentina, where he remains a bigger hero than anyone else in the country's history, including Peron and his wife Eva, the legendary tango dancer Gardel and the racing car driver Fangio. His funeral, when it comes – and many fear that will be sooner rather than later – will be bigger even than the lavish public ceremony awarded to Eva Peron. To the Argentine masses, Maradona will continue to be a source of joy and pride for years to come, a beacon of hope for a people racked by poverty and political instability.

• • •

Born in 1960, the fourth of eight children, Maradona was brought up in the suburban slums of Buenos Aires. Like so many Argentinians, his mother Tota came from an Italian immigrant family while his father Chitoro was from a rural Amerindian community in the remote north of the country. Maradona was born into a home with just enough money to feed and clothe the family, but nothing left over for anything as luxurious as a pair of football boots. In the shanty town where he grew up, crime, delinquency and hardship were a permanent feature of daily life. Football was a welcome refuge and just about the only route by which a small handful of them might escape to a better way of life.

Only once did Maradona come to serious harm as a child, when he stumbled in the dark and fell into the cesspit outside his home. He was rescued from the pool of waste by his uncle, but the incident caused him recurrent nightmares. In years to come, it would also provide journalists with a vivid metaphor for the mess he so often found himself in.

Like most kids growing up in the poorer areas of Argentina, Maradona developed a passion for football when he was very young. But unlike most of his peers, his skills quickly caught the attention of his elders. As a young boy he appeared on national television showing off his tricks, playing keepie-uppie with footballs, bottles and fruit. Even then his eyes were set on an international stage. In an early piece of footage, the young prodigy announces: 'I have two dreams – to win the World Cup and to win the [Argentinian] Championship.'

Aged ten, Maradona came on at half-time in a match between Boca Juniors and Argentinos Juniors, dazzling the crowd with his skills as great roars of admiration filled the stadium. At first glance the young Maradona didn't look like a great athlete in the making, but coaches and scouts only had to watch him for a few moments with a ball at his feet to recognize his outstanding promise. He was snapped up by Cebollitas, the youth team of First Division club Argentinos Juniors, and at just fourteen he was promoted to the club's senior set-up. In a bid to hang on to their young talent and see off potential rivals, the club wooed his family by giving them an apartment in a more comfortable area of the city. There was nothing grand about the area or the flat, but compared to the slums, the new Maradona family home was comfort itself. The set-up allowed his father to give up his filthy, exhausting job in the local animal bone-crushing factory and devote himself to looking after his eldest son's interests. During this time, Maradona received no meaningful education. His family and club were happy to let him drift out of school in order to concentrate on his career as a footballer – though that left him ill-prepared for the demands that were soon to be made of him.

In 1976, fifteen-year-old Maradona made his senior debut for Argentinos Juniors when he came on as a substitute. As he set foot on the pitch, he became the youngest player in the history of Argentinean football. His international debut came the following year, after Argentina's manager Cesar Menotti bowed to public clamour and named him among the substitutes for a friendly against Hungary at Boca Juniors' Bombonera Stadium. When Argentina went 5-1 up, the crowd started calling for his introduction. Menotti granted their wish and sent on the great new hope of Argentinean football.

Diego Maradona, already well known in football circles, quickly became a household name and the subject of frenzied media interest. By the age of nineteen he had scored a hundred goals and become a national hero. But the strains of public expectation were plain from the outset, and in several newspaper interviews he complained about the intense pressure he felt he was being put under.

Maradona was expected to play in the 1978 World Cup finals, hosted by Argentina, and making the squad became an obsession for him. When Menotti left him out, Maradona burst into tears and was plunged into a gloom that lasted for weeks. His omission would rankle with him for years and he even went so far as to threaten to quit football altogether.

General Galtieri's military dictatorship understood the benefit of associating itself with football, the people's game, particularly with the successful national team, a muscular symbol of the country's strength on the world stage. Mario Kempes may have been the star of Argentina's World Cup triumph that year, but the player everybody was talking about was Maradona, and the government was quick to exploit the rising star for propaganda purposes. Maradona, an impressionable teenager who loved his country, was wheeled out to preach the government line on the importance of conscription in the new regime and to speak of his pride in serving his country as a soldier. In the build-up to 1982 World Cup, General Galtieri went to the squad's training ground, where he was photographed hugging him.

The battle to keep Maradona in Argentina intensified as the interest from abroad grew by the month. It is a largely forgotten fact, but the first foreign club Maradona almost joined was not Barcelona or Real Madrid, Juventus or Manchester United... but Sheffield United. With former Argentina captain Antonio Rattin acting as a go-between, the negotiations were almost completed when Maradona's people decided to reject the Yorkshire club's offer. The Sheffield board refused to raise their bid for a player they had never heard of, let alone seen.

The sheer impudence of Sheffield United's bid had awoken the rest of Europe to Maradona's potential and soon there was serious interest from the Continent's leading clubs. Barcelona, the front-runners to sign him from the outset, made it clear that they were prepared to do anything it took to get their man. Negotiations between the two clubs carried on for two years, as the Argentinean authorities did everything in their power to prevent their propaganda tool from leaving the country, even subsidizing Argentinos Juniors so that they could improve Maradona's contract. Maradona's advisers, meanwhile, held out for the maximum amount of money they could squeeze out of the rich Catalan club. In early 1981 a deal was struck that would keep Maradona in Argentina until at least the 1982 World Cup finals, to be held in Spain. Boca Juniors bought him on loan from Argentinos Juniors with an option to extend his contract.

Money was now pouring into Maradona's accounts from football contracts as well as a wide range of sponsorship deals, including one with Coca-Cola. Maradona also acquired an impressive portfolio of properties, including a luxury country retreat outside Buenos Aires where he could relax with his friends and family away from the constant and intense glare of publicity. Barely out of his teens, the man with the golden feet had swapped the grime of the slums for the opulence and comfort of the penthouse suite and the country estate.

Maradona was enjoying his fame and fortune, but they also brought claustrophobic pressures to bear on him. Shortly before joining Boca, he recorded the first entry on his long criminal record when he was given a suspended sentence for punching a young fan who had hassled him for his autograph. After Boca won the championship in Maradona's first full season, negotiations with Barcelona were reopened and the Catalans finally landed him for a world record $7 million. The Spaniards would not have to wait long to see the hottest property in world football, as they prepared to stage the twelfth World Cup finals.

The reigning champions' involvement in the tournament was overshadowed by the country's war with the United Kingdom over the Falkland Islands, which had erupted in April when General Galtieri's troops had seized the tiny British-run community in the South Atlantic. The war provided the organizers with a major security problem, particularly if the Argentinians were drawn to meet England or Scotland, or even Northern Ireland, in the later stages of the competition. When the

British and Argentinean teams arrived at their team hotels they found tanks and armoured cars sitting in the car park. The war had also heightened feelings of nationalism in both countries and, particularly in Argentina, the World Cup was seen as stage on which the countries could flaunt their supposed superiority and mock their enemies. Maradona was seen as Argentina's general and standard bearer on the field, but as events turned out the 1982 finals were a humiliation both for the young star and his country.

Maradona arrived carrying not just the heavy burden of his homeland's great expectations, but also a reputation as the most gifted player in the world since Johann Cruyff. It quickly became apparent that his opponents were not going to give him the opportunity to enhance that reputation – he was kicked around like a rag doll.

He tweaked a hamstring in the week before the first game against Belgium, but recovered to play in a 1-0 defeat. Argentina went through to the second stage with wins over Hungary and El Salvador, but they failed to reach the semi-finals after defeats to eventual winners Italy (2-1) and to South American rivals Brazil (3-1). Against Italy, Maradona was battered by hard man Claudio Gentile and against the Brazilians, the mounting pressure of the tournament finally broke the young Argentinean's composure – he was sent off for kicking Batista in the testicles. (He has since claimed it was a mistake: 'I meant to get Falcao.') The dethroned champions travelled home in disgrace and the sense of national shame and impotence was compounded shortly afterwards when the country was forced to surrender the Falklands after a brief and brutal conflict. It was perhaps fitting that the two failures should go hand-in-hand in a double blow to national prestige after the military junta's desperate efforts to ingratiate itself with the country's football idols.

An angry reception party greeted the players on their return home. The squad's image wasn't helped by a string of newspaper stories and photographs showing the players and managers enjoying life to the full in their Alicante base. Maradona appeared in several photos alongside his growing entourage of family, friends and spongers, while Menotti the coach seemed more interested in enjoying life with his girlfriend than he did in coaching the squad to a second successive triumph. Football legend Pelé didn't help the Maradona cause by questioning if he had the right character qualities to be a truly great player.

• • •

Sporting a couple of days' stubble and a T-shirt, Maradona signed for Barcelona amid a great public fanfare in the capital of the semi-autonomous region of Catalonia, thus becoming the world's most expensive footballer and one of the most high-profile sportsmen on the planet. It is difficult to say when Maradona, football's golden boy, began to take wrong turnings, but what we now know for sure is that he began his near-fatal association with cocaine while he was in Barcelona. Maradona admitted as much in 1996, adding a sting to his confession by saying that he was by no means the only top footballer to have enjoyed South America's most notorious export.

To look at the man on the pitch with the ball at his feet and the opposition's defences at his mercy, no one would have known that the malevolent influence of the white powder was already starting to eat away at his body – and even more importantly, at his mind. He looked fit and he felt fit; he was only twenty-two, he was the star of one of the biggest football clubs in the world as well as one of the richest men in international sport, and a national hero to boot. The young star had lifted his beloved family out of the slums and into a life of comfort and genteel respectability. He must have known he was something special, not least because everyone kept telling him so. Why should a few lines of coke and a few beers be anything to worry about? Surely he would just sweat any after-effects off in training? He was still at that age when the body is capable of rapid regeneration.

Ironically, during his time at Barcelona Maradona appeared in an anti-drugs advert for television in which he gave some advice to youngsters: 'Do me a favour, enjoy life. When someone offers you drugs, just say no.' Maradona maintains that he was asked to grow up too quickly and that with no formal education of any consequence behind him he was catapulted into a millionaire's high life at an age when most of his peers had barely thought about a working life. There was no one in his inner circle with the strength of character to stand up to the Argentinean national hero and international superstar, no one to tell him how to conduct his lifestyle and finances in a more sensible and responsible fashion.

Maradona lived two lives in Barcelona. On the football pitch and in the changing room, his team-mates remember him as a team player, one of the lads, who never lorded it over the rest of them. But away from the Nou Camp, living in his luxury mansion with his coterie of friends and family, Maradona played lord of the manor. He had his own advisers, his own medical staff and physical training team and it was not long after his arrival at the club that this phalanx of associates began to clash with the Barcelona officials, who did not like their prize asset being looked after by what appeared to be a group of unaccountable spongers. Sparks began to fly, not least over the matter of Maradona's physical treatment. There was also growing concern over the stories sweeping the city about the all-night parties taking place at the Maradona mansion.

Maradona had a reasonably successful first season at Barcelona (1982/83), scoring twenty-two goals in all competitions, but his arrival failed to yield the prize the club so desperately craved – the Spanish league title. It was the ninth year in a row that the wealthy Catalan club had failed to land the trophy, as they trailed behind the Basques of Atletico Bilbao. The destiny of the title might have been different, however, if Maradona had not been struck down by hepatitis in December, forcing him to sit out ten weeks of the season.

In the first month of the new season, Maradona suffered the worst injury of his career when Andoni Goicoechea, aka the Butcher of Bilbao, hacked him down from behind. The Atletico Bilbao defender was banned for ten matches for his act of brutality, which left Maradona with a broken ankle and torn ligaments. A nail had to be inserted in the joint to hold it together, and Maradona was left hobbling on the sidelines for three months. The Argentinean returned to action early in 1984, but it soon became clear that the setbacks of the previous twelve months and the constant tension between Barcelona officials and his personal team were beginning to get to him.

Money problems were also starting to plague Maradona – his outgoings began to outstrip his income from advertising and sponsorship deals, which were dependent to some extent on his match fitness. Maradona wanted to get away from Barcelona anyway, but there was also the added attraction of a signing-on fee with a new club as well as a new, possibly more profitable, deal. After being substituted in one match, he burst into tears and vowed to quit the club. Maradona admitted towards the end of his career that his two-year spell at Barcelona was the unhappiest of his career – quite an admission when you consider the pile of trouble he ended up in with his next team, Napoli.

The deliverance he sought was sealed by an ugly incident in the Kings Cup final – the Spanish equivalent of the FA Cup – against

Bilbao. The rivalry between the two clubs had reached boiling point by the end of the season. The Basques had just won the league title for the second season running, fuelling Catalan frustration, while Goicoechea's tackle on their most important player at the start of the season provided a further cause for resentment.

Bilbao won the match to complete the Spanish 'double', and as Maradona walked off he was taunted by one of the Bilbao players. With King Juan Carlos looking on from the stands, Maradona responded by flattening his goader, sparking an all-out brawl between the two teams. There was outrage in the press; Barcelona did not even try to justify the reaction of their star player. By then Maradona had had a series of run-ins with Barca president Jose Luis Nunez and other club officials and was once even set upon by a group of supporters after a training session. Hailed as the man who would restore glory to the club less than two years earlier, Maradona was now *persona non grata* in Barcelona. It was time to move on.

• • •

A few weeks later, Maradona was given a tumultuous reception by 70,000 fans inside the San Pablo stadium after signing for Napoli for a new world record of nearly $10 million. When Maradona rose to national attention in Argentina, the hopes of a nation hungry for world recognition merged with the dreams of a teenage boy, and the same thing happened when he joined Napoli. The impoverished, chaotic Italian city wanted respect and recognition from its so-called superiors further north in Rome, Turin and Milan. Napoli had never won the championship and the mercurial Argentinean was seen as the man to deliver it. This was his kind of club – somewhere with an inferiority complex, with something to prove. Maradona was never at ease in the more sophisticated environment of Barcelona, but in the rough-and-tumble world of Naples he felt instantly at home.

Maradona was treated like a king by ordinary Neapolitans and it was not long before he was rubbing shoulders with members of the Camorra, the Neapolitan version of the Mafia, who exercised a powerful influence over the city at the time. He enjoyed a lavish lifestyle and soon bought himself a yacht and a fleet of cars – including a Rolls-Royce and a Ferrari. It took rather longer for Maradona to settle on the pitch, however, as Napoli struggled in the lower reaches of Serie A for the first half of the 1984/85 season. But in the new year they lost just one match and finished in a respectable eighth position. Maradona was the club's top scorer, with fourteen goals.

His second season was even more successful. Napoli finished third and showed their rivals in the north that they had become a significant force in Italian football. But trouble was brewing off the pitch, as the star's romantic life and financial affairs began to unravel. Maradona sacked his agent Jorge Cyterszpiler, a childhood friend who had run all his business affairs for nearly ten years. Cyterszpiler's company had serious cash flow problems, mainly as a result of his client's extravagance.

At the same time, Maradona was going through a difficult period with his girlfriend Claudia Villafane, his childhood sweetheart; he began to enjoy the temptations of Neapolitan nightlife and she spent more time back in Argentina. At the end of 1985 Maradona began a passionate love affair with local girl Cristina Sinagra. It had lasted for four months, until she dropped the bombshell that she was pregnant by him. Maradona immediately cut off all contact with Cristina, denying that the child was his.

There had been widespread rumours about their clandestine tryst, but when Claudia appeared on television to reveal the identity of the child's father, the news caused a sensation in Italy and Argentina, dominating newspapers, radios and television programmes for weeks. She threatened a paternity suit; Maradona continued to deny he was the father. It was an ugly situation for all parties, not least because Claudia was pregnant at the time. Sinagra gave birth to a boy whom she christened Diego Maradona Jr. Maradona Sr spent the next seven years paying lawyers to deny his responsibility before DNA tests proved him wrong. To this day Maradona has never met his son, known as Dieguito, who lives in Italy and has embarked on a promising football career of his own that has already seen him picked for the Italian Under-17 side.

• • •

Leaving behind his jilted lover and the private and public furore surrounding her pregnancy, Maradona set off to Mexico for the 1986 World Cup finals with plenty on his mind but not, it seemed, that much on his conscience.

Maradona's mental state was not the only cause for concern for Argentina at the outset of that tournament, however. The ankle so brutally mangled by Goicoechea was causing him pain and restricting his ease of his movement. The South Americans, managed by Carlos Bilardo, could ill afford to lose the one outstanding player from what, by their standards, was an otherwise mediocre squad.

With the help of painkilling injections, Maradona was declared fit to lead Argentina in their opening game against South Korea, which they won 3-1. Argentina finished top of their group after a 1-1 draw with Italy and a 2-0 win over Bulgaria and then progressed to the quarter-finals with a 1-0 win over South American neighbours Uruguay in the last sixteen matches. That victory left them facing England in a match that the Mexican security forces feared more than any other.

The memory of the Falklands War still weighed heavily on the hearts and minds of the Argentinean people; their swift and crushing defeat by the former imperial power was regarded by many as a national humiliation played out before the eyes of a crowing world. There was no diplomatic contact and little commercial co-operation between the two countries. Now they were to be represented in an entirely different type of battle, in an event bursting with symbolism. A victory would allow Argentinians to feel as if they had somehow avenged their military rout; defeat would plunge the country into greater despair. The match attracted one of the biggest television audiences of the entire tournament and it turned out to be one of the most dramatic and controversial contests since the tournament began fifty-six years earlier.

In the sweltering afternoon heat of Mexico City, the contest exploded into life with one of the most hotly disputed goals in the history of football. England's Steve Hodge sliced his clearance from the edge of England's area and the ball looped back over his head. Maradona stole into the box but, being one foot shorter than Peter Shilton, he appeared to present little danger as the England goalkeeper advanced off his line to collect the ball. Maradona sprang up as Shilton reached out with both arms for what seemed a relatively simple take, but a split second later the ball had been squirted into the back of the net. At first it seemed as if the Argentinean had somehow managed to get a head to the ball, but television replays soon revealed that it had been an entirely different part of the Maradona anatomy that had put the South Americans in front. In the blur of rising bodies Maradona could be seen lifting his left arm slightly above his face and discreetly palming the ball downwards and into the net. Asked about the incident after the match, Maradona said that if there had been a hand involved then it must have been the hand of God. (A nice conceit, that: 'You all saw it was my hand, therefore I am God.')

Today, Maradona is unrepentant about his cheating. 'I was happy, I am happy and I always will be happy with the goal I scored with my hand,' he says. 'All I can do is offer the English a thousand apologies, but I'd do it again. As a boy of five or ten I used to score goals with my hands in the minor leagues and I continued to do it when I played in the [Argentinean] First Division.

'In Argentina, a "carterista" is a pickpocket. They get on a crowded bus, bump into people and steal their wallets. That's what I did to the English – I stole their wallet without them realizing. Argentinians are proud because no one saw me. They identify with that.'

Five minutes after delivering that first shock, Maradona struck again, but this time it was with a goal of sublime beauty that left even Englishmen open-mouthed with admiration. Setting off from the half-way mark he skipped past and danced round half the England team before poking the ball into the net, sliding towards Shilton at full pelt. BBC commentator Barry Davies spoke for 25 million disappointed Englishmen watching back home when he conceded: 'You have to say that was magnificent.'

England introduced John Barnes, who put a marvellous cross into the penalty area for Gary Lineker to score from close range, but it was too little too late. The Argentinians held out for a victory that many regarded not just as the greatest moment in football, but as one of the greatest moments in the country's entire history. Argentinean radio commentator Victor Hugo Morales, who covered the match, says today: 'The England game was something special. All us journalists in Mexico said it had nothing to do with war, but we knew we were kidding ourselves. We Argentinians had a great need to defeat the English in that game. When we beat England – thanks to Diego, with the cheek of his first goal and the artistic beauty of his second – the country exploded with pleasure, satisfaction and revenge.'

At the time Maradona played down the Falklands factor, but today he speaks differently. 'It was as if we had beaten a country, not just a football team,' he says. 'Although we had said before the game that football had nothing to do with the Malvinas war, we knew they had killed a lot of Argentinean boys there, killed them like little birds. And this was revenge.'

Inspired by Maradona, Argentina went on to beat Belgium in the semi-final and then to win the trophy with a 3-2 win over West Germany. It was an extraordinary triumph for both player and country, considering Maradona's problems off the pitch and the mediocrity of the team he was playing in. 'Pride in this country reached its peak in 1986 thanks to Diego,' says Morales. 'Nothing compared to winning the World Cup in 1986. Many Argentinean fans are unemployed or are poorly paid. They lose every day of their lives and only have the possibility of winning on Sundays through football. So when the national team wins, it's like beating the whole world, showing that we are superior to another country. The player who gave us that feeling most often was Diego Armando Maradona.'

After returning to a heroes' reception in Buenos Aires, Maradona and the rest of the squad were invited to the Casa Rosada, the governmental palace, by President Raul Alfonsin. Maradona held the trophy aloft from the balcony, but this was very much Alfonsin's photo opportunity, not Maradona's. The president was basking in the footballer's reflected glory.

• • •

The following season, Napoli were crowned champions for the first time in their history, prompting a week-long party in the city during which normal life ground to a halt. Maradona, the club's top scorer again that season, was central to their success, and Napoli also lifted the Coppa Italia. The twelve months from the World Cup triumph in Mexico to Napoli's 'double' success in Italy would prove to be the peak of his career. From there the only way was down – and Maradona didn't take the scenic route. His life slid into chaos on almost every front: professional, financial, medical, moral and emotional.

Inevitably, Maradona had been drawn into the shady Neapolitan underworld run by the Camorra. As the most famous man in the city and one of the world's great footballers it was almost impossible to avoid contact with the powerful figures who played such an influential role in the life of the city. Maradona's association with Napoli's less wholesome citizens would ultimately lead to a major police investigation into his activities.

In 1988, injuries returned to plague him, placing further strain on a relationship with his employers that was already stretched by the tug-of-war between the club's officials and Maradona's 'people'. His absences from training became more frequent and many fans started to lose patience with him, feeling that he was not rewarding their love and support for him. When he hobbled out of one match in 1989, the fans jeered him and Maradona reacted with characteristic fury. Reports in local and national newspapers suggested that the star was enjoying himself too much off the pitch and not looking after himself physically.

The abuse of his body, much of it self-inflicted, was beginning to catch up with Maradona. He had been receiving painkilling and cortisone injections for over ten years during which, week in week out, he had been kicked like a bucket by desperate defenders unable to cope with his superior skill. Maradona found himself in the vicious circle that so often besets footballers with a taste for the high life – his increasingly frequent absences through injury gave him plenty of time to indulge himself and get out of shape.

Maradona's stardom, however, showed no sign of dimming back in Argentina. His marriage to Claudia Villafane in 1989, a riot of extravagant kitsch in Buenos Aires Cathedral, was the social event of the decade. Over 1,400 guests were invited, many of them flown in from Europe on a specially chartered jumbo jet, to witness the world's greatest footballer wed his childhood sweetheart. Cristina Sinagra and her son Diego Maradona Jr were not on the invitation list.

In 1990, Napoli won their second championship, but Maradona's contribution to the triumph was negligible compared to his efforts three years earlier. His form and popularity in Naples may have been fading, but by the start of the 1990 World Cup in Italy, Argentinean expectations of their idol had once again reached a feverish level as the country prepared to defend their title. Just as they had been four years earlier, Argentina were an unexceptional team with one truly great player in their midst. Italy, Germany, Holland and Brazil – and, some would argue, England – were stronger on paper. But Argentina somehow managed to reach the final for the third time in four competitions before losing 1-0 in an ugly contest against a West Germany side who, inspired by Lothar Matthaus, avenged their defeat in the final in Mexico.

By common consent, Argentina were lucky to have got anywhere near the final, particularly after losing to Cameroon in a bruising curtain-raiser to the competition. The South Americans scraped into the knockout phase after finishing third in a group of four, following a win over the Soviet Union and a draw with Romania. They were an unpopular team with few obvious charms or merits and even Maradona failed to shine. His most significant contribution to the Argentinean cause came when he provided the pass for Claudio Caniggia to score the winning goal against Brazil in the second round. Penalty shoot-out wins over Yugoslavia in the quarters, then the hosts Italy (in Naples) in the last four, saw Maradona's side squeeze into the final, where they were finally found out by a typically well-organized, tough German side. An Andreas Brehme penalty settled a dull match that did little to enhance the sport's reputation, with Argentina having two players sent off. Nor had seven matches on the biggest stage in international sport done much to check the mounting suspicion that the world had probably seen the best of the stocky Argentinean.

Maradona had blown the opportunity provided by Italia '90 to put himself back into the front of football's shop window and improve his chances of a lucrative transfer to a new team where he could relaunch his flagging club career. But far worse was to follow in 1991 when he was arrested and charged with the consumption and distribution of a class A narcotic: cocaine. Maradona's off-pitch activities had fallen under greater scrutiny following a police campaign against organized crime. Both he and a friend were investigated at length by the police in connection with major clampdowns on rackets involving drugs and prostitutes. In Italy, where libel law is regarded as something that happens only in other countries, papers ran sensational stories about Maradona as a string of women came forward to claim that they had had sex with him and to give details of wild parties, orgies and drug-taking.

Newspapers love nothing more than a story of a fallen idol, and stories of the former World Player of the Year's disgrace filled thousands of column inches around the globe. Maradona was banned from all competitions for fifteen months and his fragile world collapsed in on itself. The flood of stories, true or otherwise, spelled the end of

Maradona's turbulent seven-year spell in Naples, even though it would be two years before the club could offload its former star player. He may have become damaged goods, but as far as the money men at Napoli were concerned his market value might rise again and they weren't going to release him if there was any chance of getting some more return on their world record investment. If he had still been delivering on the pitch at the time of the drugs revelations, Napoli might well have shown greater public support for the Argentinean, but his form had slumped and he was now more of a liability than a valuable asset. Far from standing by him, Napoli even tested him for drugs themselves after one match (he tested positive for cocaine).

Maradona was nearing the end of his career as it was, and any hopes of a money-spinning final transfer to a major club were fast disappearing. Sponsors and advertisers were quick to dissociate themselves from a man who would only tarnish the image of their product. Deals with Coke had been wrecked by coke deals. Furthermore, Maradona's track record had shown that he had a tendency to indulge himself during an injury lay-off and now, with a year and three months to kill, only the most fervent optimist could have expected him to curl up in front of the fire with a boxed set of Gabriel Garcia Márquez novels after a daily workout in the gym.

Former Argentina coach Cesar Luis Menotti says the ban made no sense. 'FIFA made a big mistake by suspending him and taking him away from football,' Menotti maintains. 'It was a disgrace. It was as if someone had stopped Mozart from playing the piano because he took drugs. Even today Maradona can't bear to be an ex-player. So it was a great shock to him when he was suspended in Italy for a year. The only thing that you cannot take from a man is his dreams, and I believe that for Diego that suspension was the beginning of the end.'

Maradona headed back to Argentina to escape the blinding searchlights of public scrutiny in Europe, but if he was looking for refuge there, he was to be disappointed. A few weeks after his return police raided a flat he had lent to a friend and found Maradona semi-conscious and sprawled on a bed with cocaine next to him after a party.

Diego Armando Maradona was at his lowest ebb. Drugs were wreaking havoc with his body, his mind and his career; his marital life was under severe strain; his financial problems were worsening; his marketing contracts were being shredded; and he was putting on weight. His life was a mess. Besieged by the media, and with his reputation at an all-time low, Maradona was under virtual house arrest as he tried to disappear from public life. Psychologists were called in to help pull him out of the vicious downward spiral he was in, but Maradona was not interested in facing up to any painful truths. He remained entirely unrepentant and cast himself as the innocent victim of 'the authorities'. It is a measure of the unimpeachable esteem in which he is held by ordinary Argentinians that many of them took to the streets to protest his arrest and show their support for him. Shortly after news of the arrest hit the streets of Buenos Aires, groups of supporters turned up at the police station to cheer him.

Maradona started a rehabilitation course in an effort to piece his shattered life back together, and by the end of 1992 he had recovered sufficiently for Bilardo, now manager of Spanish club Sevilla, to help arrange his transfer from Napoli to the modest Spanish club. Maradona's fans rejoiced that he appeared to have surmounted his personal problems and returned to action, but their joy – and his – was to be short-lived. Maradona was a shadow of the player who used to have the world of football at his feet, and a blazing row with Bilardo in the changing room brought to an end another unhappy chapter in his recent life story.

Maradona's problems were now feeding on themselves with a voracity that would push lesser men to the brink of insanity. Not long after the Sevilla fiasco came to an end in 1993, the DNA tests ordered by an Italian court confirmed Cristina Sinagra's boy had been fathered by Maradona. After seven years of denial and evasion, there could now be no hiding from the truth.

In February 1994, Maradona snapped. Besieged by a posse of reporters and photographers outside his country villa in Moreno, the troubled player opened fire with an air rifle, injuring five of them. He was arrested and charged but it took four years for the trial to come court. The former World Cup captain was sentenced to more than two years in jail in 1998 for the shooting, but the prison term was suspended. In a separate trial brought by one of the victims, Maradona was also ordered to pay a substantial sum of damages after the judge ruled that his privacy had not been infringed at the moment of the attack.

Today, Maradona remains magnificently unrepentant about the incident. 'Let's be straight about this,' he argues. 'If there are helicopters with journalists and photographers above your house and your daughters come running to you saying, "Papa we can't swim because the water is being disturbed" – yes, then I become a terrorist. I'm a terrorist when they upset my daughters. No one touches my daughters. For twenty years I earned money chasing a ball so today my daughters can have what they want. If they harmed my daughters – say one of the helicopters crashed on them – what would happen? I'd have to spend all my money finding all the journalists that were there as well as all their families. Then with a grenade in my hand I'd bid them all goodbye and then kill them. Whoever touches my daughters dies.'

The shooting incident, which was filmed by television crews, failed to silence the growing clamour amongst Argentinean fans for their hero to be included in the national squad for the 1994 World Cup finals in the United States. Far from being pilloried by the public or punished by the football authorities after his air-rifle attack, Maradona's standing was almost enhanced by the incident. His supporters saw his actions as an inevitable and justifiable reaction to the intense strain placed on him by an intrusive media. Three months earlier, Maradona had joined Newells Old Boys, one of Argentina's best-known clubs, in an effort to get himself somewhere near match-fit, and he was considered to be in good enough shape to captain Argentina and secure their place in the finals with a 2-1 victory against Australia over a two-legged play-off.

Maradona's physical appearance at the start of the tournament suggested that he had indeed finally cleaned up his act. The thirty-three-year-old had committed himself to a drastic regime in a desperate bid to lose weight and he looked lean, muscular and bursting with energy as he practised before the world's camera crews in Argentina's training sessions. All the puffiness had gone from his face and he seemed relaxed and in good spirits.

Maradona played in Argentina's first two group games against Nigeria and then Greece, against whom he scored a superb goal. His celebration of that goal became the most enduring image of the tournament and led to a string of jokes about his recreational drug habits. As the ball hit the back of the net, Maradona wheeled away to the camera positioned at the side of the pitch and pushed his face into the lens with a look of such wild ferocity and dementia that it had the world's armchair fans diving for cover under the cushions. 'God is back in business,' seemed to be the message that the Argentinean captain was trying to convey to the international community.

That moment, though, proved to be Maradona's last hurrah on the world stage. He promptly found himself embroiled in a fresh drugs scandal after testing positive for a cocktail of banned ephedrine substances. On hearing the results he burst into tears – as did half of Argentina, when news of yet another sorry episode in the life of their most notorious son hit the streets back home.

Maradona's personal fitness instructor had allegedly given him some over-the-counter drugs for a cold, medication that he had bought when the team were in Boston. But FIFA and the World Cup organizers, desperate not to have the image of their product degraded by association with drugs cheats, were taking no chances. They threw Maradona out of the tournament and for the second time in his career he was banned from football for fifteen months. His friend Adrian Paenza recalled the moment he heard the news: 'I was in the room half an hour after he learned he was banned from the World Cup. And when he saw me, he came over and hugged me. He was crying so badly. I had never seen anyone cry that badly except when someone in the family had died. He was absolutely devastated. He wouldn't let go of me.'

To Maradona's friends, this episode was just one more example of the football authorities' two-faced attitude to the world's best player. He was hailed when it suited them to bask in his reflected popularity, but he was alienated, damned, rebuked and left to rot when his personal problems overwhelmed him.

Maradona claimed conspiracy by the football authorities. 'They've cut my legs off,' he told reporters. FIFA later conceded that although he had been in breach of doping rules, Maradona had not deliberately drugged himself. But by then it was too late. His reputation and career had been wrecked once and for all. Maradona was branded a disgrace – again – by the world's press. Unsurprisingly, the man himself doesn't see it that way. 'No. In Argentina you can't talk about a footballer being a disgrace,' he argues. 'In Argentina, the disappeared were a disgrace, the Falklands was a disgrace. It's a disgrace the way we are robbed every time we vote. I'm not the disgrace of Argentina – quite the opposite.'

The most remarkable aspect of the whole episode was that the Argentinean authorities did not monitor Maradona more closely to ensure that no rogue substances found their way into his body. The problem was that Maradona was virtually untouchable. Nobody told the hero of the people what to do.

• • •

Maradona's final drugs shame marked the end of his remarkable playing career, although he didn't officially announce his retirement until 1997. Subsequently, he did at least try to rebuild a meaningful career in football, the only world he knew, but his attempts at club management with two Argentinean sides were brief and unsuccessful. He also started an international players union with his spiritual bedfellow Eric Cantona, the *enfant terrible* of French football, but that had become a white elephant almost as soon as he had walked out of the press conference in Paris to launch it.

Without the clear focus and direction that comes with life as a professional footballer, Maradona sought out alternative thrills and his life began to drift, deprived of the adrenaline rush of competitive action in packed stadiums and before worldwide television audiences. Speculation about the state of his health had been rife for years but, in January 2000, Maradona was taken to intensive care in Uruguay after suffering heart problems. The first medical bulletins said he was suffering from hypertension and irregular heartbeats, but subsequent tests showed evidence of heavy cocaine use.

Today, Maradona denies that recreational drugs were the cause of his collapse, echoing his claims after testing positive at the World Cup in 1994 that it had been an over-the-counter cough remedy, mixed with sleeping pills, that had triggered the attack. 'I was woken by this great pressure on my chest,' he recalls. 'I lay down and I began to cough. I wanted to sleep but I couldn't relax, I was too tense. I got up and saw my face was swollen. I was frightened. But it wasn't a drugs problem. The problem was that I had mixed cough medicine with sleeping pills. I hadn't been taking drugs – not then. I admit I have taken drugs, but I swear on my daughters' lives that I hadn't that night.'

'I'd be lying if I said it [cocaine] hadn't hurt me,' Maradona told a Channel 4 documentary crew in 2001. 'Because of it I've gone days without seeing my daughters, and they're the most important thing to me. I don't struggle to return to football. I struggle for more important things that the drugs didn't take away from me, and that's my feelings for my daughters. Anyone who says different can answer to me. I'm not lost. My daughters are my reason for living – with drugs, without drugs, with football, without football.'

Maradona was ordered to rest and relax, but the pictures of him after his release showed him to be obese and virtually impossible to recognize as the same man who, fourteen years earlier, had skipped through half the England team in Mexico City to score that sensational one-man goal.

He was just forty, but he had the heart of a seventy-year-old – a heart that doctors said was virtually at a standstill when he arrived at a health spa in Cuba as a guest of Fidel Castro to begin his latest reha-bilitation course. 'Commandant Castro came to see me in person to confirm what the newspapers have been saying: that Cuba is my country. He and all Cubans are praying for my speedy recovery,' Maradona told the British film crew allowed to join him at the spa. Doctors in Cuba said that only 38 per cent of Maradona's heart tissue was functioning at the start of 2000, but after five months of rehab he was well enough to start exercising again.

He was allowed one day off from his programme during that period and when the film crew followed him to a friend's barbecue one Sunday, they returned with some footage that would have given his doctor a heart attack of his own. Clearly making the most of his one day's escape from his strict regime, the man his team-mates used to call 'Fatty' at the outset of his career, was filmed eating enough red meat to satisfy a pride of lions, with plenty left over for the hyenas and the vultures. Washing it down with several bottles of beer, Maradona sat back with a giant Havana cigar to watch his beloved Boca Juniors play rivals River Plate on television. If Maradona was worried about the state of his health, it was certainly very difficult to tell from watching him hop up and down screaming blue murder at the television: 'Son of a bitch! Queer! F**king son of a bitch!' Even the heart of a man in the best of health might have struggled to keep going under that kind of exertion.

Maradona survived the barbecue to complete his rehabilitation course and return to something resembling normal life. His battle against drugs will doubtless be a life-long struggle, but he was given a goal to focus on when it was announced that a testimonial between an Argentina XI and a World XI at the Bombonera would be staged in his honour. The prospect of the match would help concentrate his mind on keeping his nose clean and encourage him to look after his body. No one, least of all the star of the night, wanted the tribute to turn into a freak show.

Despite his retreat from public life, Maradona has continued to make the headlines. Late in 2000 he returned to Italy to collect his FIFA-sponsored Player of the Century award, on a night made memorable by the continuation of an ongoing and unedifying spat with Pelé. The simmering row between the two great players erupted once again following the publication of the results of FIFA's Internet poll. Pelé, almost universally accepted by the 'experts' as the most complete, gifted player the world has ever seen, polled a miserable 18 per cent of the worldwide vote, while Maradona clocked up a staggering 54 per cent. FIFA had opted for a voting system that was painfully vulnerable to abuse – if one person with access to the Internet had felt strongly enough about it, it was perfectly possible that Steve Bruce might have been voted football's Player of the Century. The Brazilians got wind that Maradona was on course for a landslide win and lodged an angry protest with the world governing body. FIFA quickly fudged a compromise by holding a second, parallel vote for coaches, journalists and their own officials. The awards ceremony was designed as a celebration of world football, but long before guests had swallowed their first vol-au-vent and drained their first glass of Moët Chandon, the entire affair had descended into farce.

On the night itself, Maradona was whisked away in a cavalcade of Mercedes from Rome airport with his wife and two daughters, mother, father, brother and manager. After collecting his award, he walked straight out of the gala event, in what was seen as a snub to Pelé, who was yet to accept his award.

Maradona made no comment to the press, but Pelé was happy to talk. 'It's true we are not good friends,' said the Brazilian. 'He was a good player and I have respect for him, but if he thinks he was the better player of the century, that's his problem.'

A couple of months earlier, Maradona stirred things up by alleging that Pelé had enjoyed a homosexual experience with a coach of a junior team. Maradona was accused of jealousy and envy by Pelé's circle of friends and associates, one of whom, Celso Grellet, suggested El Diego had been deeply upset that former Argentinean president Carlos Menem had invited Pelé to Argentina as special guest because he was his favourite player.

In his autobiography *Yo Soy El Diego*, Maradona lists Pelé as number one in the list of his favourite hundred players, but as he patted him on the back with one hand he delivered a low punch to the midriff with the other, with the following comment: 'As a player he had it all, but didn't make the most of it to raise the status of football. I'd like to see him put himself forward as president of an association to defend players' rights – like I did. I'd like to have seen him look after Garrincha and not let him die in misery. I'd like to see him fight the rich and powerful that are damaging football.'

Maradona continues the battle to rebuild his life, but he can take comfort from that fact that he has always remained a national hero in Argentina. The tribute song 'Le Mano de Dios' still blares out of radios up and down the country, while his face still stares out from a thousand billboards and magazine racks.

His testimonial match went ahead as planned towards the end of 2001, with a full Argentine team plus Maradona taking on an array of stars from past and present and featuring other former international bad boys Cantona, Hristo Stoichkov and the eccentric Colombian goalkeeper Rene Higuita. Maradona barely broke into a trot, leaving all the running first to his compatriots and then to the tears that streamed down his face as he addressed the crowd in what became an emotionally charged occasion. Even Pelé was in the crowd to pay tribute to the man he freely admits to disliking. 'He deserves a testimonial for all the happiness he has given people,' acknowledged the Brazilian. 'It's important for me to be present.'

Maradona has always loved a challenge, but now he faces the biggest of his life – to dodge an early death and find a new passion to replace the football and narcotics. Given his association with drugs and his history of temperamental outbursts, football clubs are unlikely to employ him as coach despite his charisma, player-pulling power and undoubted inspirational qualities. But Maradona, stubborn as a mule, continues to dream of more glory in the football stadium. 'I've reached a point where I want to work,' he told the British film crew during his rehabilitation in Cuba. 'I dream of coaching Manchester United or Barcelona or Real Madrid or Boca Juniors. I'm on medication now, but I won't be drugged up like a zombie because that's not a life. I'd like to work because it would help me not think about drugs. The problem is, no one would employ someone who takes drugs. It's discrimination, but they'll never kill my dream.'

Though he has not yet gone to that great football pitch in the sky, Maradona's ghost haunts Argentinean football. 'El Diego Es Eterno' read the banners as the country's stadiums echo to the chant of his name even when he is thousands of miles away. El Diego himself finds it difficult to overstate the symbiotic relationship between Maradona and the Argentinean people. 'I am not Diego Armando Maradona. I am "El Diego" for the Argentinians,' he says. 'I belong to every Argentinean who has smiled or cried for me, through the good times and the bad, right up to today.'

Maradona was not put on this world to solve its problems, only to make people feel a bit better about their lives through the magic and beauty of his football. He happened to be born with a gift to do almost supernatural things with a football, in a poor country where football provides one of the few stages on which the nation can compete with the best in the world. At the age of fourteen, Maradona became the standard bearer of his people's hopes and their yearning for respect, and it is impossible to measure the weight of that responsibility or to understand the temptations and extraordinary pressures that gradually led him into a world of drugs, crime and scandal. An early death would turn him into a legend: the Marilyn Monroe, Elvis Presley or James Dean of the football world; an outrageous talent who died young. His friend Adrian Paenza believes that for many, Maradona's premature death would the perfect end to an incredible life story: 'Actually I think that people are waiting for him to die. That would wrap up the whole thing. Then the story would be closed.'

GEORGE BEST

IF HE COULD PASS A BAR LIKE HE COULD PASS A FOOTBALL...

'George was the greatest footballer who ever played the game. He was just a fantastic athlete. He was the quickest, the strongest, he had the most endurance, he could tackle, shoot, use both feet, he was brave, he had a great engine, he had a good head, he could pass and he scored millions of goals. What more do you want in a footballer?'

Rodney Marsh

Off the pitch, the greatest footballer ever born in the British Isles was as striking as he was on it. Dubbed 'the fifth Beatle', the drop-shopping handsome Best was football's first pop star, a pin-up for girls, an idol to men and boys alike, the lover of hundreds of beautiful women and the owner of the most expensive and sought-after body in world football.

Best had everything going for him – even a superlative name that a cartoon sketch writer might have invented. But like all tragic heroes, the Ulsterman had one great flaw. Best's was the tankard… or the champagne flute… or the wine glass… or the brandy balloon… or the sherry glass. And his unquenchable thirst for alcohol has come within a glass or two of killing him. In March 2000 Best admitted himself to the private Cromwell Hospital in West London. Football's premier sex god had become a bloated and yellow parody of his former self, his face was horribly blotched and he was doubled up in agony. His liver was all but destroyed and his spirit was hanging by a few threads, haunted by his craving. Deprived of alcohol – the one constant in his helter-skelter life – Best has battled to recover what is left of his world and his future.

Never has there been a footballer, certainly not from these islands, who has been such an inspiration to aspiring young footballers and yet such a vivid advertisement of the perils and pressures of fame – not to mention the dangers of alcohol abuse. Best's greatness as a footballer is matched only by his vulnerability as a man. Genial, shy, good-natured, generous and humorous, Best could not be fairly depicted as a villain. He is a troubled soul, a tortured genius, with all the flaws we hope our heroes never have.

• • •

Born in 1946 in Belfast into a Protestant family and community, George Best's gift for football was first spotted when he played for a local team, Cregagh Boys. Bob Bishop, Manchester United's long-serving scout in Ulster, sent Sir Matt Busby a telegram that read simply: 'I've found you a genius.' Best did not look like a natural athlete, as he was unusually skinny by anyone's standards – let alone the standards of an aspiring professional footballer. 'He was so slight it looked as if you could blow him over,' former United coach and manager Wilf

McGuinness recalls. The frailty of the Best frame led to early rejections by local Northern Irish clubs and then by Leeds, all of whom failed to notice that the skinny lad with all the tricks possessed an essential quality for a great footballer: balance.

Best went to Old Trafford at the age of fifteen, but United nearly lost him, thanks to their attitude on his arrival. Today, it's unthinkable that a club would let a young teenager, away from home for the first time, make his own way to its ground after stepping off the boat in Liverpool, thirty miles down the road. But that's exactly what United did. Best was soon homesick, and with no one at the club seeming to care whether he was there or not, he ran away back to Belfast. His father Dickie rebuked United for their careless treatment of his son, but after a few weeks of gentle coaxing he persuaded his boy to give it another go.

Best was soon causing something of a stir. Aged seventeen, he was called into the first team, making an unprecedented leap from the junior to the senior side without the customary bedding-in period in the reserves. He made his professional debut in 1963, against West Bromwich Albion, drawing a handful of appreciative notices in the press. Best quickly found his feet in England's top flight, showing no signs of self-doubt as he gave a string of hard-bitten fullbacks the run-around down the flanks. The young prodigy had balance, timing and outrageous skill by the bucketload and it soon became apparent that his size barely mattered, because if he was shoulder-barged, he would bounce right back up. If someone tried to chop him in half, the precocious young Belfast boy would skip over his assailant and leave him sitting on his backside in the mud.

Best's first truly spell-binding performance came against Chelsea at the start of the 1964/65 season. He was so good that at the end of the match the entire crowd at Stamford Bridge applauded him off the field. The legend was born.

'He never became a big man physically,' observes United defender David Sadler, Best's close friend and room-mate for many years in the digs provided by the club. 'But the inner strength of the man was incredible.' Best himself remembers the worries about his weight. 'The first game I played for United I think they thought I was the ball boy,' he says now. 'I must have weighed about eight stone. I was never nervous about playing, but I was a bit apprehensive about it because I was so light. But I found out very quickly that I had the one thing that most great athletes had, and that's great balance. Over my career I very rarely got hurt. I got knocks and bruises, but nothing serious. I never broke anything. And besides, I could look after myself.'

Best was heavily right-footed when he first began juggling with footballs, but after watching Real Madrid's Francisco Gento warming up at Old Trafford, playing off both feet with equal dexterity and composure, he determined that he too would become equally proficient with both his boots. By the time he was eighteen, there was no way of telling which was his stronger foot. He was the complete player.

Naturally, opposition teams came to bury Best, not to praise him. Dave Sadler remembers the physical punishment the young player suffered from a generation of defenders unable to cope with his skill and desperate not to be humiliated by this Irish upstart. 'He had lumps kicked out of him,' Sadler recalls. 'The only way they could get close to him was to kick him. He had some horrendous treatment. But in a funny way, he loved all that. He was a bit like a matador with a cape. He would want to go back and do it again to them because these animals were trying to maim him.'

Best, though, wasn't hanging back waiting to be crippled by a ruthless opponent. He loved the physical challenge of the game almost as much as the more artistic contributions he was expected to make. Sir Matt Busby always maintained that Best was the best tackler at United. 'George Best was gifted with more natural ability than any other player I have seen,' Busby enthused. 'He was also enormously courageous and had more confidence in his ability than any other sportsman I have known.'

If Best had a weakness as a player, it was that he would hang on to the ball for too long. McGuinness, who took over from Sir Matt Busby for a brief and unhappy spell as United's manager, notes: 'The thing he liked most was the ball and when he got it he wouldn't give it to anyone.' He could be a selfish player and often drove his team-mates to distraction. Bobby Charlton and Denis Law were particularly frustrated by Best's mazy dribbling. Law was the star of the show until Best casually trotted into the limelight, whereupon his goals began to dry up. Law was used to getting the ball on demand, but when he was in the mood, Best gave the impression that his team-mates were irrelevant.

As Best and United went from strength to strength, winning the league title in 1965, the youngster's wage packet swelled and the advertising contracts started to mount. With more money than he could ever have dreamt of when he first stepped off the ferry from Northern Ireland, Best's lifestyle began to change. Nights out at the bowling alley with his mates from the youth team were swapped for early evening trips to the pubs and late night bars after hours. To start with, there did not appear to be anything for United – or for him – to get too alarmed about, because he was still producing on the pitch and the training ground. He was incredibly fit and his young body could easily shake off the alcohol the following morning. But even in those early days there were signs that self-discipline was going to be a problem. In the 1965/66 season he received his first punishment from the club when he was fined and suspended for three matches after a couple of late nights.

If the match against Chelsea had awoken the nation to Best's outrageous gifts, United's 5-1 European Cup quarter-final win at mighty Benfica catapulted him to stardom. Benfica were regarded as the best team in Europe at the time and the morning after their demolition, Best was mobbed outside his hotel room. Men sought his autograph while girls screamed and jostled for a lock of his hair. 'That was the match which put him on the map,' affirms McGuinness. 'That made him a star not just in this country but also in Europe. All of a sudden George became a pop star. Crowds of women – married women as well! – were chasing him. It was unique. I am sure the majority of men would have been the same as George with all these gorgeous girls chasing him...'

With his mop of black hair and dark good looks, Best soon became known as 'the fifth Beatle'. 'In his prime he was stunning looking,' remembers Mike Summerbee, his rival at Manchester City but one of his close friends and drinking partners off the pitch. 'Everyone just loved George Best at this time,' confirms Bobby Charlton. 'This adulation had never happened before; no one had been put into the spotlight as a footballer. It was phenomenal.' Best opened his own clothes boutique and appeared in countless advertising campaigns, for products ranging from oranges to women's bras. 'Suddenly the guy was on the sports pages, the news pages, the fashion pages – he couldn't move without it being reported,' says Sadler.

But the 1965/66 season was to have a painful end for Best. Two weeks after his mercurial display against Benfica, he suffered a career-threatening knee injury playing against Preston in the FA Cup, but the operation for the injury was delayed so that he could play against Partisan Belgrade in the European Cup semi-finals. Manchester United lost the tie and Best suffered permanent damage to the cartilage in his knee that has dogged him ever since.

By the start of the following season, George Best was spending almost every night of the week out on the town, drinking a good deal – though nothing like as much as he would a couple of years down the line. He was also seen out with as many women as he could lay his hands on. Not surprisingly, United were starting to worry about Best's wild lifestyle of booze 'n' birds. But they couldn't criticize his dedication on the training ground, where he was still regarded as the most committed of players. When the rest of the squad had gone in for a shower, Best would invariably stay out, practising some aspect of his game that he felt needed improvement.

George Best has been linked to a string of beautiful women throughout a tempestuous romantic career. 'He might have been a womanizer but he never behaved like a cad,' says the singer Lynsey De Paul, one of his early high-profile conquests. 'He was always charismatic and charming.' Best, who claims to have bedded seven women in one night, says simply: 'I think I'm just a normal bloke. I love the company of beautiful women and I like to be seen with them... I also enjoy the company of my pals just as much. But [the papers] don't write about that, me going out with my mates from the shipyards.'

By the time he was twenty years old, Best was a vodka drinker. He drank for all sorts of reasons: for fun, to overcome his innate shyness, to blot out pressures of his sudden fame and because his celebrity dragged him into a glitzy showbiz world. Once all the wine bars and regular pubs were shut for the night, Best and his small group of friends – often including Mike Summerbee – would move on to some of Manchester's less salubrious joints. Part of the problem was that Best was caught between two social circles at United in those early years. He was the youngest player in the team and many of his team-mates were married or had serious girlfriends, so he rarely fraternized with them. His early promotion to the senior side, meanwhile, meant he became more distant from his peers in the junior teams. As a result, his group of close friends was soon made up of people outside football: entrepreneurs and businessmen who could afford the same expensive lifestyle as him. It was a worrying development as far as United were concerned. Moreover, he didn't have a proper home. For most of his time at United, Best lived in 'digs' in a modest boarding house. With thousands of pounds in his wallet, nationwide celebrity and half the female population trying to sleep with him, Best was never likely to be the sort to go back to his room, read a book and get an early night...

• • •

Although he couldn't have realized it at the time, the year 1968 would mark the peak of George Best's career. He was only twenty-two, but it would all be downhill from here. 'You felt it was going to be our year,' says Best. United would finish the year as European champions, the first English side to win the Continent's premier club competition, and Best would be named European Footballer of the Year. The European Cup Final was played at Wembley against Eusebio's Benfica, the team United had destroyed two seasons earlier. The game didn't come to life until extra time, both teams erring on the side of caution, but United seemed to be heading for victory when Bobby Charlton headed them in front, only for the Portuguese to level nine minutes from time. Benfica had the chance to kill the game, but thanks to keeper Alex

Stepney the match went to extra time and within a minute Best had dribbled past two defenders and left the keeper for dead to fire United in front. Brian Kidd, on his nineteenth birthday, added the third goal and Charlton the fourth.

For Matt Busby it was an especially emotional occasion. Ten years earlier he had been involved in the Munich air crash, which took the lives of eight of his brilliant young team on their way back from Belgrade after a European Cup semi-final match. The team was poised to dominate English football for a decade to come and Busby, who carried the physical and psychological scars of that ordeal to his grave, set about rebuilding it. That night in Wembley was the reward for his courage and determination. But for Best, one of the biggest nights in the history of English football is now just a blur. 'I can't remember anything about after the game,' he admits. 'The last thing I recall was Sir Matt and his smiling face, coming onto the pitch and hugging me. The rest is a total blank and I can't remember where we celebrated or who with. Nothing.'

The 1968 European Cup Final was George Best's finest moment. The accident of his birth meant that he would never grace the international stage in a meaningful competition. Northern Ireland had a handful of players from the English First Division, but they were basically a very ordinary side, the majority of the squad coming from the Second and Third divisions and semi-professional local teams. Best never played in the World Cup finals or European Championship and only rarely shone on international duty. Part of the problem was that he was used to playing with world-class players at United. He would lay on the same kind of passes as he did for his club, but his Irish team-mates lacked the speed or the vision to run onto them and Best would end up getting jeered for making what looked like a bad pass.

By the time he had lifted the European Cup that May night, alcohol had become a major player in George Best's life as the pressure of his fame began to bear down on him. 'The intrusions had already started,' he recalls. 'It was one thing having your photo taken for magazines and modelling, but when it comes to people parking outside twenty-four hours a day and making up stories about you, that's over the top.' Best had become a tabloid news editor's dream: good looking, brilliant at football, living a life of champagne, beautiful women and fast cars (a white, chauffeur-driven Jag was his preferred mode of transport). The tabloids helped build him up; now they were going to give him a good kicking on the way down.

Best admits today that he used the pressures of his fame, as well as the slow decline of the United side after 1968, as an excuse for his heavy drinking. Unprecedentedly, he now began to skip training and even to miss the train for matches. Sometimes he would disappear for days on end, launching into major drinking binges with the same gusto he had once applied to his training. Bobby Charlton, English football's shining, squeaky-clean knight of the realm, was flabbergasted by Best's lifestyle. (The two of them didn't get on until well into middle age.) 'I remember going around the training ground with him once and him telling me about his lifestyle and I simply couldn't believe it. How could he play football after that, I thought?'

Best has always insisted that perhaps only twice in his career did he ever go drinking the night before a match. Thursday, fine, but not Saturday. 'You simply can't play, and stories that I turned up and played matches half-cut are just ridiculous,' he insists. 'You would be sick all over the pitch.' As Best's life began to spin out of control, his friends – and there were a lot of them – tried to steer him back onto the straight and narrow. But he didn't want to know. Rodney

Marsh tried to take him aside once and was told to 'Fuck off and mind your own fucking business.' Malcolm Wagner, a Manchester businessman, says all Best's close friends had tried to counsel him. 'We would try and say to him: 'Why stay out till five when you can leave here at two o'clock?' But he would just glaze over when you gave him advice.'

By the time he reached twenty, Best's closest friends were night-club and bar owners and he was earning £3,000 per week, an astro-nomical sum of money for the day. Would things have turned out differently if he had been more strictly monitored by the club? It's diffi-cult to imagine Sir Alex Ferguson tolerating such rampant hedonism, even from such a prodigiously talented player. Indeed, before Sir Matt Busby died, he questioned whether he had been too soft and indul-gent with him. If George Best had been kept in cotton wool until the initial euphoria mellowed into quiet admiration, might he have stayed on course? Had he become a carpenter, say, would he still have made the same mistakes? Or was he destined from birth to self-destruct? The problem for Best was that while he was having a wonderful play-boy time and feeling terrific on the pitch, physically and emotionally he was already doomed.

Best quickly became disillusioned with life at United after the great achievement of 1968. After Busby's retirement at the end of the following season, an ageing team went slowly downhill; no big names were brought in to replace the likes of Bobby Charlton, Denis Law and Pat Crerand. A power vacuum had developed after Busby became United's general manager and McGuinness was asked to take over as coach. It was a poisoned chalice. None of the players knew who was truly in charge and the affable McGuinness became the fall guy for the club's accelerating decline. McGuinness still feels let down by Busby, whom he believes didn't do enough to quell a players' revolt. He found the experience so stressful that his hair fell out.

'I think the worst thing was that we didn't strengthen the team and George began to feel he was doing everything himself,' reflects McGuinness. For the first time since he began kicking footballs as a toddler, Best was disillusioned with the game. 'There was no Denis Law, no Bobby Charlton, no Pat Crerand,' he says now. 'It was becoming like a job to me, like I was just clocking in every morning.'

To compensate for the lack of excitement on the pitch, Best hit the booze and the casinos in a big way. 'If George had a drink, it never ended,' explains Barry Fry, Best's team-mate in the United youth side. 'If George had a gamble it never ended. If George had a woman it never ended. It was all or nothing with George Best.' Best played the field off the pitch, as it were, but according to his friends he was always in search of a permanent partner. 'He bed-hopped because it was available, but if he could find the right one he would stick with her,' affirms Malcolm Wagner.

Fame, fortune and 40 million pints were quickly addling Best's judgement. On a pre-season tour to Denmark, the United team were relaxing in a Copenhagen bar during training when a beautiful woman came in. McGuinness picks up the story: 'There were not many bra-less women around in those days and when she walked through the door I saw George's eyes follow her across the room and I thought, "He's going to arrange something with her."'

The woman was accompanied by her powerfully built boyfriend that evening, so Best did nothing at the time, but on his return to England, he took out adverts in Danish newspapers to track her down; she would later be dubbed 'the Striking Viking' by the papers. Eva Haraldsted was picked out from hundreds of applicants and she came to live with Best in Manchester. The relationship got off to a bad start after a first-night misunderstanding about Eva's role in Best's life; it became very clear early on that she was not prepared to just lie back in El Beatle's boudoir and think of Denmark. 'The first evening we didn't really succeed because he was thinking differently,' recalls Eva, a little embarrassed now about her encounter with Ulster's greatest Lothario. 'He thought I was just a girl like all the others.'

For Best, the episode is best forgotten – 'She thought we were going to get married and I didn't.' He broke off the relationship not long after and she sued him for breach of promise, a first in English law. 'It was no big deal,' says Best. 'I gave her some money [£500] and she went out with a friend of mine for a while and then went back to Scandinavia.'

Not one to do things by half, Best also had affairs with two Miss Worlds. The first, with the American Marjorie Wallace, ended in embarrassing acrimony when she accused him of stealing a fur coat, her passport, some jewellery and a cheque book. Best was arrested but the case against him was finally dropped. 'I think it was pretty obvious to everyone that I didn't take anything,' he comments, dismissively. In another farcical episode that did little for his standing at United, Best went AWOL for days before he was tracked down to the north London flat of the actress Sinead Cusack, where he remained holed up while the British press corps camped on the front door. When he finally emerged and returned to Old Trafford, Busby suspended him for two weeks and fined him two weeks' wages.

George Best's life was becoming a steamy soap opera to which the nation was glued. But behind the superficial glamour of his life, darker forces were at work. Alcohol was no longer just a recreation, a welcome diversion from the publicity. Best had slid into a downward spiral: the booze undermined his playing, while the pressure on him and the criticism of his performances increased, so he turned back to the bottle for comfort. His absences from training became more frequent, as did his failure to keep appointments. He even failed to turn up for Bobby Charlton's testimonial match, preferring to stay in the pub getting drunk a few miles down the road from the match at Old Trafford.

When the Troubles erupted in Northern Ireland in the early 1970s, Best found himself dragged into the terror. He needed a police guard after he received death threats from the IRA and his fears were heightened when a woman reported seeing a man outside his house with a gun. The threats to his life plunged Best into a state of despair, fuelled by alcohol. He was sent to see a psychiatrist, but he merely laughed at his questions, just as Diego Maradona would twenty-five years later.

Heading into what should have been his best years as a player – his mid- to late twenties, Best announced his retirement at the end of the 1972 season and picked up a substantial cheque from the newspaper that ran his full story. But football's golden boy was nothing if not mercurial. By midsummer he had had a change of heart and was back at United in pre-season training. In a bid to straighten out his lifestyle the club urged him to move in with Paddy Crerand and his family. The plan worked for less than a week before Best returned to his favourite watering holes. With his playing on the slide, George started to expand his horizons beyond the beautiful game, opening the first of several clubs, Slack Alice's, in the centre of Manchester.

United and Best had gone into decline hand-in-hand at the start of the decade and both finally collapsed. The 1972/73 season was a disaster for United. Frank O'Farrell, McGuinness's successor, was sacked and the colourful Scotsman Tommy Docherty took over.

United's fall from grace was perfectly reflected in the increasingly wayward behaviour of their star player, who found himself being constantly fined and suspended by the club for skipping training and going on all-night benders. A string of incidents involving Best, including one in which he was accused of hitting a girl in a nightclub, brought unwelcome publicity for the club and unneeded distraction from sorting out the problems on the pitch. United could no longer tolerate their unruly, wilful prodigal son and in a move that would have been unthinkable on that sultry night at Wembley five years earlier, the former European Footballer of the Year was sacked.

At the end of the season, Best had his first serious brush with death – and alcohol had nothing directly to do with it. He was on his annual summer holiday in Spain when the lower half of his leg swelled up like a balloon. A local doctor gave him some pills and sprayed the swelling, telling him it would soon disappear, but Best was not convinced and called his doctor in Manchester. He got on a plane to come back, sweating, twitching in agony and fearing for his life. 'I was frightened to death,' he states, flatly. His friend Malcolm Wagner was there to meet him at the other end. 'We met him at Manchester airport on the tarmac,' remembers Wagner. 'He was put in an ambulance and rushed straight to hospital. It was thrombosis and if it had moved it would have killed him.'

Best made a full recovery, but the incident shocked him into sorting out his health and he launched himself into an intensive fitness programme. At the start of the season Docherty invited him back to Manchester United. Best was seriously overweight at the time but by late October he was fit enough to play and he was given a hero's welcome when he ran out at Old Trafford again. But two months later, the United love affair was over once and for all. Docherty claimed that

Best turned up drunk with a girl on his arm before an FA Cup tie at Plymouth in early January and that he refused to let him play. To this day Best disputes Docherty's accusations. He makes no attempt to hide his loathing for Docherty, who would leave United in disgrace a few years later after an affair with the wife of the club's physiotherapist. 'I didn't like him as a person,' says Best. 'They were a poor team and got relegated. I didn't want to be a part of it.'

And, effectively, that was it. There would be a dozen comebacks but George Best's life as a serious footballer had now ended. 'When he left Manchester United, his career was over,' says Marsh. 'He was a European Champion, European Player of the Year, he had won the Golden Boot. You can't get higher than that. He had done everything. When he left Man United, there was nowhere to go.'

Neatly closing the book on a colourful and turbulent era for the club, United were relegated at the end of the 1974 season. The coup de grace was delivered by none other than their former hero Denis Law, now playing for their detested neighbours Manchester City.

Henceforth, Best became a footballer-for-hire, playing for a bewildering array of clubs over the next ten years. And the first port of call for the former European Footballer of the Year? Dunstable, a footballing backwater struggling at the bottom of the First Division South of the Southern League. Dunstable were managed by Barry Fry, who called his old friend Best on the wild off-chance that he could be persuaded to trot out for them in a few home games. The arrangement would assume a familiar pattern over the next few years. Struggling club pays Best lump sum to appear in home games. Gate receipts double or treble. Best trots around the pitch, a shadow of his former great self. Fans grow disillusioned. Novelty wears off. Best moves on.

'As a manager I knew it was a great coup,' admits Fry. 'He was far, far, far too good for me. He was on another planet. He should have been gracing the best grounds in the world.' Soon afterwards Best had a brief pay-as-you-play spell at Stockport in the Fourth Division before, at last, a club with a decent reputation – Chelsea – came in for him... only for the deal to collapse because the London club were in deep financial trouble and couldn't meet Best's demands. After a short stopover playing for Cork in the Irish League, he flew to the United States, where the Major Soccer League had recently been launched, backed by millions of dollars. Eager to get away from his troubles back in England, Best was only too happy to join the migration of ageing stars – including Pelé and Beckenbauer – as well as the non-entity journeymen queuing up for the cash, the sunshine and some of the least demanding football of their careers.

Early in 1976 Best signed for the Los Angeles Aztecs. 'It seemed perfect,' he remembers. 'America was very exciting, to start with. Some of the best players in the world were there and there were massive crowds. I had about seven years there and it was fabulous.' Well, perhaps, but Dave Sadler, his old room-mate back at United, was just one of many old friends who had mixed feelings about Best's career, hopping back and forth across the Atlantic. 'At least he was playing, I thought,' Sadler says, 'but it was all a bit of a circus.'

At first the American experience seemed to straighten out Best, giving him a new lease of life without the suffocating pressure of life in England. Former Manchester City midfielder Bobby McAlinden, who played with Best at the Aztecs, recalls that Best threw himself into another heavy fitness programme. 'When he arrived in America, he wasn't in top shape, but nor was he in particularly bad shape,' says McAlinden. 'He was maybe a stone overweight. But he really worked on the physical side.'

Best was soon as fit and happy as he had been since his early days at Manchester United. The booze was under control. He looked and felt great. 'I did leave behind everything because no one knew who I was,' he says. 'I could walk out the front door and know that no one was going to jump out from behind a tree or get me with a zoom lens from half a mile away. It was so relaxing.' He felt good enough and was playing well enough to come back to England and sign a contract with Fulham, then in the Second Division, joining Bobby Moore and Rodney Marsh at the sleepy London club on the banks of the Thames. But after some early success on the pitch, playing to full houses, Best once again found himself making headlines for all the wrong reasons. He was fined and suspended for making a 'wanker' gesture at opposition fans, and his drinking was getting out of control again. Best's waywardness almost killed him after one particularly heavy day on the bottle, when he smashed his car into a lamppost outside Harrods and went through the windscreen. He was taken to hospital and given fifty-eight stitches.

Seeking a new life across the Atlantic for a second time, Best rejoined the Aztecs in September 1977. But soon after his return he began to struggle when the knee he had damaged irreparably in 1966 started playing up again. 'I started getting a lot of fluid on the knee because the pitches out there were so hard,' he explains. 'I had to drain my knee before games and afterwards it was always very sore.' Bobby McAlinden says the problem was a constant source of discomfort for the former prodigy. 'He still can't walk properly today because of it,' he reveals 'It was always very swollen. Watching him drain it was bad enough – heaven knows what it must have felt like.'

In 1978 Best married Angie Janes, his English girlfriend of eighteen months, at a time when his life had fallen into chaos. The wedding ceremony in Las Vegas, which took just three minutes, summed up the entire marriage: a catastrophe wrecked by alcohol. Best was drunk as he gave his vows and had to borrow a ring from his best man after forgetting to buy the symbol of his supposedly everlasting commitment to his wife.

His football life wasn't much better. Fed up with his frequent absences and his drinking benders, the Aztecs offloaded Best to the Fort Lauderdale Strikers in Florida. Fulham, who still held his registration, objected to the move and appealed to FIFA, who imposed a global ban on Best. The day after having his livelihood taken away from him, he was hit by a second, even more shattering blow. His beloved mother Ann died, emaciated by alcohol, at the age of fifty-four, just fourteen years after having her first drink. Best was devastated by the news and with the perverse logic of the alcoholic, sought comfort in the bottle.

Best finds it difficult to talk about his mother these days without welling up. He loved her and is racked by guilt that he was not there at her side more often towards the end of her life. In addition to the natural love of a son for his mother, Best as a fellow alcoholic, also knew the horrible physical pain and inner anguish Ann would have felt after becoming addicted to drink. 'She's someone you always thought was going to be there. And to be on the other side of the world when it happens and to have to come back and deal with it, it's pretty difficult...'

When the global ban on him was lifted in 1979, Best played a few more games for Fort Lauderdale before a very public falling out with English coach Ron Newman. He was suspended and hit the bottle even harder, prompting Angie to walk out on him. The snubs and setbacks were now raining down on him. His finances were a mess, and back in England Manchester United denied him a testimonial on the dubious grounds that he had not been at Old Trafford for more than ten years. True, he had been there just a few months less than the statutory period, but other players had been granted a testimonial without serving the full ten years, and Best was knocked back by what he saw as the club's mean-spiritedness.

Still trying to ply the only trade he knew, Best went to Edinburgh to play for Hibernian in late 1979. As before, the first few home gates were huge before quickly tailing away as the fans realized that the bearded figure lumbering along their touchline was not the Messiah they had been praying for. Best was overweight, unfit, living in a hotel, drinking heavily and demonstrably uninterested in playing for the poorest team in the Scottish top flight.

He was soon on the move again, this time to San José Earthquake. His career there could not have got off to a worse start: he opted to miss his first press conference and go on a four-day drinking binge instead. By now, George Best's personal life was in a tailspin. He later admitted that matters were so bad around this time that he stooped to stealing money out of a woman's purse in a bar when she went to the toilet. Angie was powerless to arrest his increasingly dangerous commitment to the bottle. She hid his car keys, drugged his coffee so he would fall asleep and once even hit him on the head with a plank to try and knock him out. All to no avail.

Best was now regularly embarking on five-day binges, when the only thing to pass his lips was alcohol. He went downhill fast, but when he hit the bottom he finally decided to do something about the problem that had dogged his life for nearly fifteen years. He checked into the Vesper Hospital for a group therapy rehabilitation course.

M.B. Wilder, one of the people to treat Best at Vesper, feels that the player must have carried a lot of psychological weight around with him on the pitch: 'He must have felt he was pulling an anchor after him when he was playing – the hangovers, the mental fuzziness, the funny feelings of failed obligations – all that must have been a lot of extra work.' Jeff Manchester, Best's personal counsellor at Vesper, believed fame was a major contributing factor to his addiction. 'George's fame had disastrous consequences,' he insists. 'The press, the parties – if there was anything *designed* to interfere with anyone trying to get sober, it was a life like that. If you're a bartender, then fine, you can go get another job.'

Best's life now read like the script for a screen drunk and the hazy world he lived in was becoming a dark cartoon. Back in London, he was attacked by a stranger in a pub on the Kings Road and needed dozens of stitches. Rodney Marsh was amazed by the endless series of scrapes his old mucking partner was ending up in. 'Every day there was a George Best story,' he recalls. 'And it wasn't, "George Best opens a supermarket" or "George Best goes to a birthday party with his baby", it was "George Best smashes his Jaguar through the window at Harrods."'

In 1982, Best got involved with his second Miss World, Mary Stavin, while he was still married to Angie (they didn't divorce for another four years). The affair with Mary lasted only a year before she walked out, exhausted by his lifestyle. And if that wasn't enough, Best's financial problems were now also mounting and he was declared bankrupt over unpaid income tax.

In late 1984 he failed to appear in court on a drink/drive charge and the magistrate dispatched the police to bring him in. George was in bed sleeping off a drinking binge, having been released from police custody a few hours earlier. Hearing there was a warrant out for his arrest, Best slipped away on another pub crawl and when the police finally caught up with him, dozens of officers bundled him into a back of van with the Ulsterman kicking, flailing punches and swearing blue murder. Once in the van, Best claims one of the officers called him an 'Irish wanker', prompting one of the best headers of a ball of his generation to lean forward and headbutt his abuser. Best says the other officers leapt on him, battering his body but leaving his face untouched so there would be no evidence of brutality in court. The magistrate had absolutely no sympathy for the fallen idol, however. Best was close to fainting when he was ordered to serve three months, courtesy of Her Majesty. 'The first part was horrendous,' he recalls, 'because it was over Christmas and New Year and I was in Pentonville.'

By now, George Best's world had completely collapsed around him. His career was over, he was bankrupt, he was in prison, his body was racked by abuse, his mother was dead and he knew that his insatiable craving for alcohol would never ever go away. To his credit, though, he used prison to get himself in shape physically again. There were more temptations inside than outside, but Best spurned the drugs – and for the most part the booze – as he struggled valiantly to get his life straightened out. When he came out, he seemed to have reformed. With new love Mary Shatila organizing his life for him, Best joined the after-dinner circuit, slowly overcoming his natural shyness to become a moderate success in his new field.

But the ghosts of his craving kept returning to haunt him. His life soon became a predictable cycle of heavy drinking followed by painful periods trying to dry out. It got so bad that when he finally collapsed in bed after a binge, he would have to sleep with a bottle at his bedside in case he felt the thirst when he awoke.

Eric Cantona putting one over Leeds, the club that helped relaunch his career.

Cantona and Blackburn Rovers'
Colin Hendry at work.

The catwalk king modelling for
Paco Rabanne in Paris in 1993.

Frank McAvennie enjoyed one remarkable season at
Celtic before his career went downhill.

McAvennie in his natural habitat – surrounded by glamorous women.

Diego Maradona, the greatest player of his generation, remains a hero in Argentina despite a string of scandals.

Maradona leaves Italy's hard man Claudio Gentile for dead in the 1982 World Cup.

George Best is sent off playing for Northern Ireland against Scotland in 1970.

George Best in 1972, wearing the Manchester United strip,
and in 1998, still battling his demons.

Stuart Pearce surges upfield in England's 1990 World Cup group game against Egypt.

Pearce would spill blood more than once for Forest and England.

A dejected Pearce following his infamous missed penalty against West Germany.

Brian Clough was a prolific goalscorer for Sunderland
before injury ended his playing career.

Clough salutes the crowd at the City ground
towards the end of his colourful reign at Forest.

Wimbledon's Vinnie Jones gives Villa the verbals.

What, me, guv?
Vinnie in trouble again at Chelsea.

Hollywood, 1999. Jones hits town.

Alex Ferguson shows off his silverware at Aberdeen.

Sir Alex signing autographs for Manchester United
fans at the opening of the club's megastore.

As his public star waned and newspaper editors no longer got excited every time someone rang in with an 'I saw George Best having a drunken row' story, Best got on with the battle to stop drinking. He was involved in a drunken brawl in Tramp nightclub in London's West End, following a row over a former girlfriend who was there with Tim Jeffries. But his public image took an even greater battering on a deeply embarrassing episode of *Wogan*, the BBC chatshow, in 1990. 'So what happened to the man Pelé called the world's greatest footballer?' asked the eponymous host. 'Let's find out...' Best, who had drunk himself daft in BBC hospitality, staggered on set wearing a lurid green shirt, grinning from ear to ear, with his eyelids at half-mast. For the first part of the interview, he mumbled incoherently about the parlous state of modern-day football. Then Wogan asked him how he chose to spend his time these days. 'Terry, I like screwing,' came the reply. And with that, Wogan, with the air of a kindly vicar, declared: 'Ladies and Gentleman, Mr George Best!' whereupon the nation's one-time idol was quickly bundled back to the hospitality suite. Best's alcoholism was no secret, but this very public humiliation brought home to millions the extent of his fall from grace.

'If you're an alcoholic, you're an alcoholic. From birth,' insists Best. 'When alcohol starts controlling you, rather than you it, that's when you know you've got a problem.' Best has spent the past ten years battling to control his alcohol problem and he has been helped along the way by his current wife Alex, whom he met in 1994. He has won several of his battles with the booze, but the war has always been going the way of his enemy. In March 2000, he was rushed to hospital with a liver like an oversized, pickled walnut and a body on the verge of total collapse. Only a small percentage of his liver was still working and doctors told him later that a few more drinks might have killed him. 'He was in so much pain,' says Alex. 'And the more pain he was in, the more he was drinking. I just wanted to get him into hospital.'

He was there for eight weeks, his body no longer able to process the buckets of poison he had been pouring into himself for over thirty years. Professor Roger Williams, a liver specialist who treated Best at the Cromwell Hospital, recalls: 'He was very yellow, very ill indeed.' After his release Best headed to Northern Ireland and set up a new home in a fishing village, away – he hoped – from the temptations that could end his life. The advice Best received was simplicity itself. 'Professor Williams said "stop or die",' says Best. 'If it was just me, then fine, but there are too many others to consider. If it was just me, then I would probably say "Screw it, I don't care."'

Publicans were urged not to serve him, but shortly after his release from hospital rumours swept through Belfast that Best had died. His agent Phil Hughes, who represents his idol for free, recalls hearing the news: 'We heard these rumours and at first you're a little worried and I called him non-stop. But I knew it wasn't true. If George Best is dead you don't get a call from the guy on the desk at the BBC – it's going to be screamed all over the world.'

Best underwent a controversial operation at the Cromwell Hospital in a final bid to stop his habit and give him some chance of a longer life. Antabuse pellets, designed to make him violently ill if he had a drink, were sewn into walls of his stomach. If he managed to hold down more than one, the chemical reaction would probably kill him. 'It is a radical operation,' says Professor Williams. 'Because the pellets are put in under the skin. They are there and you can't take them out. A chemical substance is being released all the time.'

Best was counselled about the dangers of the operation, which is relatively common in Scandinavia. It is impossible to drink owing to the violence of the reaction and so the pressure switches to the patient's mind and soul. You have to be strong in spirit to survive because there is no longer the bottle to run to. You are a prisoner of the pellets. 'It's an operation they don't like doing and you have to go through assessments with psychologists to make sure that, mentally, you know what you're in for,' says Best. 'They've only done it to three or four people in this country.'

George Best faces a painful struggle for the rest of his life with his health in a constant state of jeopardy. The craving will never abate. 'They can control you, drugs and alcohol, and you just cross your fingers and you hope you're one of the lucky ones. But it's not over till you die – only then do you know you're not going to have another drink again.'

Thousands of column inches have been written about the sadness of George Best's decline, but Rodney Marsh, one of his closest friends, believes we should celebrate his life, not pity and patronize him. 'What really pisses me off is when I hear people say, "What a tragedy George Best the human being is",' Marsh fumes. 'It's nonsense. George Best knows exactly what he's doing. He's a very intelligent, bright man and he knows the penalties for what he's doing and it's his choice. All these Samaritans and do-good people that criticize him – that's bollocks. Because George Best knows his destiny. He knows what he's doing.'

They wish him well, this skinny Ulsterman who brought them such happiness through the magic of his boots.

HARD MEN

STUART PEARCE

HARD AS NAILS

They call him Psycho, short for psychopath. A dictionary definition of 'psychopath' reads: 'a person who shows a pathological degree of specific emotional instability without specific mental disorder; someone suffering from a behavioural disorder resulting in inability to form personal relationships and indifference to or ignorance of their obligations to society, often manifested by antisocial behaviour such as acts of violence or sexual perversion.' By that definition, 'Psycho' couldn't be more inappropriate...

Stuart Pearce is one of the hardest, most passionate and most patriotic players ever to pull a football shirt over his head. But he is also one of the most controlled, self-disciplined, fairest and universally respected footballers around. Even the tricky wingers he has spent twenty years dismantling and bulldozing have never accused of him of foul or violent play. Pearce hates cheats. He thinks football is a man's game to be played with honour and dignity. If someone is foolish enough to trespass against this god of the terraces, he will have his retribution. But it will be justice, not revenge, he metes out on the wrongdoer, and it will all be by the book, as Pearce calmly walks back into position, having delivered a painful lesson in what it means to be truly hard on a football pitch. 'He's got one hell of a lot of aggression inside him – but it's all under control,' explains former England manager Terry Venables.

It's been said that when you're tackled by Stuart Pearce, you stay tackled – and there is almost certainly not a right-winger in English or international football who would argue with that – let alone argue with the man himself. You don't mess with Stuart Pearce, white van man in a football shirt with the three lions of England scalded onto his heart.

Pearce is a throwback to an earlier football era, when players treated their game as a job; a player cast from the same mould as Tommy Smith, Norman Hunter, Billy Bremner, Graeme Souness and Ron 'Chopper' Harris. You can kick him, you can punch him and you can head-butt him, but Stuart Pearce will just get up again, football's equivalent of the Terminator steaming back at you with a deranged look in his eyes.

Away from the pitch, Pearce is a model professional, a family man and probably the only top England footballer of the last generation not to have been subjected to the 'exclusive' treatment in the front half of the nation's tabloids. There ain't no dirt on Psycho.

But Pearce is one of a dying breed. It won't be long before players like him vanish from the game altogether as FIFA slowly clamps down on tackling. There are some high up in the sport's world governing body who want to ban tackling altogether – enjoy him while he lasts.

•••

In an era of football celebrity, players can seem removed from the public who pay to watch them – but not Stuart Pearce. As far as the fans are concerned, he's one of them on the pitch, with pride, patriotism and commitment to the cause evident in his every gesture. 'I know it may sound funny, but I love Stuart Pearce loads. If you pay your money to see a football match, you want to see someone on the pitch giving it you back and Stuart Pearce gives it back loads,' says England fan Ashley White.

Unlike most top footballers of the last generation, Pearce didn't learn his trade in one of the country's elite academies, but on the bloody and brutal killing fields of non-league football. His senior career began as a semi-professional with Wealdstone and Dynamo Kingsbury Kiev, a Sunday pub team. 'That was my breeding ground,' he recalls. 'You see everything in non-league football, fights down the tunnel, the lot. My attitude has always been, "I don't care if at the end of ninety minutes my opponent hates my guts." I really, really don't care.'

Stuart Pearce was born in Hammersmith, London, the youngest by ten years of four children. His mother was a dinner lady at the primary school he attended and his father was a waiter in the West End and later became a postman. As a teenager growing up in west London in the late 1970s, Pearce developed a love for punk music that remains to this day. He has seen The Stranglers over forty times, he treasures a drumstick given to him by the drummer of Stiff Little Fingers and you can spot him in a crowd scene on the cover of a Lurkers album. He even introduced the Sex Pistols' 'Filthy Lucre' tour comeback gig in Finsbury Park in 1996. He never got a punk haircut, but he did wear pyjamas to concerts. Although he was mixing with a fairly rowdy crowd, he managed to steer clear of trouble for the most part. He had three minor brushes with the law, all of them the result of heavy nights in the pub with his mates, which resulted in criminal convictions for stealing a car, being drunk and disorderly, and criminal damage (after climbing a set of traffic lights).

Pearce never imagined that he would end up playing in the top football division, let alone for England. Rejected by Queens Park Rangers, the team he supported as a boy, Pearce went for job interviews with the police and the Army before opting to learn his trade as an electrician. He passed all his exams and soon secured a full-time job with Brent Council. Back in those early days, Pearce's confidence in his playing ability was low: as far as he was concerned, he was a tradesman who was quite good at football.

Then, in 1983, Pearce was given his big break by Bobby Gould, Coventry's manager at the time, who bought him for £25,000. Most players rise up through club youth teams or work their way up the division, but Pearce's transfer to Coventry marked a rare instance of a player making the huge step-up from non-league football into the toughest division in world football.

Pearce spent two seasons with the Light Blues before Brian Clough, the most revered manager in English football back then, called him up and invited him to join Nottingham Forest. Pearce had no hesitation in accepting the offer, and it was at the City Ground, on the banks of the Trent that he spent his prime playing years. It only took a few months at Nottingham Forest for Pearce to earn the nickname Psycho. One tackle in particular awoke English football fans to the fact that there was a man of almost maniacal commitment to the cause in their midst. Chelsea's Pat Nevin, one of the most skilful wingers in English football in the early 1980s, received the ball wide on the right. All seemed right with his world for a split second, as he prepared to set off on a mazy run. Then, in a flash of red and white, a football meteor in the form of Pearce came hurtling out of nowhere, 12 stone of solid, flying muscle, and virtually cut the little Scotsman in half. Nevin turned over once and lay crumpled on the turf. The crowd took a collective sharp inhalation of breath and Pearce backed away. 'Today you'd expect GBH charges against him,' says John Barnes. 'It was like beauty and the beast, with Nevin the beauty and Pearce the beast.'

Pearce is the ultimate journeyman player made good. He is unique in modern football in that he is the only top player to have kept his trade while playing football in the first division, as it was then known. He may have been an ex-punk rocker, but he was a long way from being irresponsible or reckless about his livelihood and his prospects. He even advertised as an electrician in the Forest match programme while he was captain of the team. Clough would often bring in his household appliances for Pearce to repair and get him round to his house to sort out any wiring problems.

Pearce had a workmanlike relationship with Clough in two respects. Clough, the unpredictable maverick of the dugout, could be a difficult person to get on with and several players couldn't handle his eccentricities and volatility. But Pearce didn't take any of his rantings personally, accepting the man for what he was – a wayward football genius who could claim to be one of the greatest managers the English game has ever seen. When Pearce was named in the full England squad for the first time, Clough called him into his office and told him he wasn't good enough to represent his country. Other players might have wilted in the face of such confidence-crushing comments, but Pearce simply set about proving him wrong.

There was never any doubt about the awe in which Pearce was held by the club's followers, though. Over 24,000 fans filled the ground for his testimonial match against Newcastle, more than had turned up for the FA Cup quarter-final match against Midlands rivals Aston Villa a few months earlier. Clough's working relationship with his loyal captain would end in acrimony after Pearce felt put out by Clough's refusal to discuss the renewal of his contract. Pearce ignored his manager for the rest of the season, at the end of which Forest were relegated and Clough left the club. No one, except Stuart Pearce, had the balls to blank him.

Pearce's introduction to international football couldn't have been more daunting. His first cap came against Brazil in 1987 and was immediately followed by games against Scotland and West Germany – in other words, the best team in the world followed by England's two most hated rivals. Playing against the Brazilians at Wembley, Pearce gave the wider world a glimpse of his almost preternatural toughness. He threw himself into a 50-50 ball with Josima, forcefully but fairly, while the Brazilian's challenge was ugly and bordering on criminal, scraping his studs down Pearce's outstretched shins. It was a tackle to turn the stomach. 'I was five yards away and I was fearful for him,' says Barnes. 'I thought he must have broken his leg. But Stuart Pearce just got up and walked away, and it was Josima who had to go off because he twisted his ankle. It was the worst tackle I had ever seen, but Stuart didn't even flinch.'

Bobby Robson, the national manager at the time, was quick to see the qualities of mental and physical toughness Pearce would bring to the side. 'He shook people up,' says Robson. 'You could almost see the three lions on his chest. He was proud of his shirt and he gave everything he had.' Pearce was a member of an extremely strong England team that built up a powerful momentum and reached the semi-finals of the 1990 World Cup. England's exit at the hands of West Germany on penalties was a painful experience for the whole squad and all follow-ers of the national team – but particularly for Pearce. The Nottingham Forest defender gave away the free kick that led to Germany's fluke opening goal in the 1-1 draw, but worse was to follow in the penalty shoot-out after the teams remained deadlocked in extra time.

'I knew Stuart would be one of the five to take a penalty and we were more nervous than ever,' says his wife Liz Pearce, who was watching the match in the Turin crowd alongside Stuart's parents Dennis and Lil. It was 3-3, Lineker, Beardsley and Platt all having slot-ted home their spot kicks, when Pearce made the long walk upfield from the centre circle to take England's fourth with half the world watching on television and every German in the crowd catcalling his approach. Whoever went through to the final would be outright favourite to take the most coveted trophy in world sport – they'd be facing an Argentinean team that most experts, including their own, considered to be uncharacteristically mediocre.

'You're fatigued and you're under huge pressure,' recalls Pearce. 'I took penalties for my club, but I think anyone who steps up to take a penalty will have a doubt in his mind. I don't care what they say. And the bigger the occasion, the bigger the doubt. You're extremely nerv-ous walking up to take that penalty. The worst bit of it is the walk-up from the centre circle. I don't know who invented it, but all I know is that it's a long walk up there and a hell of a lot longer on the way back if you've missed it.

'You hear the crowd as you're walking up, you hear the crowd when you're putting the ball down and then you walk back and are getting focused and you don't hear a thing any more.'

As far as Robson was concerned, Pearce was an automatic choice for the shoot-out. 'Stuart Pearce, in my opinion, was our best penalty taker,' he says. 'In training, he just used to wham them, burst the net. So I decided that Pearce should be our number four. All penalties in a shoot-out are crucial, but to my mind number four is the most crucial. Often it makes or breaks.'

Pearce calmly placed the ball, like all penalty takers, right at the front of the white spot and then turned around purposefully and walked back for his run-up. 'I always fancied my chances of scoring a penalty. I've always preferred to have the responsibility than leave it someone else.'

'I had made my mind up long before the game that if I had a penalty I was going to smash it down the middle,' he reveals. That's exactly what he did. Smash it down the middle, hard and low – but not quite low enough. Bodo Illgner flung himself to his right, guessing completely wrongly, but his exceptionally long legs were left trailing in mid-air and Pearce's ferocious cannonball of a strike thundered into the goalkeeper's feet and away from the net.

'Obviously, you think, "This is it. My penalty's knocked us out."' Pearce looked as if someone had hit him over the head with a plank. He stood there dazed and then began his slow trudge back to his devastated team-mates in the centre circle with the sound of German celebrations reverberating in his ears. Gary Lineker was the first of many to put his arm around the big man's shoulders. Back amongst his team-mates, Pearce could not bring himself to look any of them in the eye. Instead, he squatted like a wounded animal, a towel around his neck, his head in his hands, sobbing. It was the first time he had ever cried on a football pitch. These were not Gazza tears, the tears of a young, volatile maverick who wept when he was booked earlier in the match, meaning that he would have been ruled out of the final. These were the tears of the most controlled, hardened player of his generation, the tears of a man who thought he alone had somehow betrayed the country he loved so much.

'You feel guilty you have let the whole country down. Liz was there and so were my mum and dad,' recalls Pearce. His wife Liz remembers the occasion well: 'I couldn't actually see him crying at the time but I saw it later on television and I felt devastated for him.'

Olaf Thon scored for Germany to make it 4-3 before Chris Waddle blasted his penalty, the fifth, so far over the bar you would have thought he was Rob Andrew at Twickenham. Pearce, though, refuses to accept that Waddle had anything to do with England's exit. As far as he was concerned, it was all of his own making. It was just as painful for manager Bobby Robson, who knew that England had come within an inch or two of making a final they would have been favourites to win. 'I felt complete and utter devastation. My whole life just went out of my body. I'll never, ever forget it,' he says now.

As Pearce left the field, head down, trying to hide his tears, Thomas Berthold asked him to swap shirts. 'Not here, mate,' Pearce told him. 'I'll do it in the dressing-room, but I'm not walking off this pitch with a German shirt on.' When Berthold came into the dressing-room a few minutes later, someone told him to 'f**k off', but Pearce got to his feet and handed over his shirt.

Emotionally drained and surrounded by celebrating Germans, Pearce was to suffer a final ignominy when he became one of the two England players chosen for a random drugs test. All he wanted to do was get out of the stadium, the scene of his greatest humiliation as a footballer, and commiserate with Liz and his team-mates. Peter Shilton was the other player chosen to give a sample, and as a goal-keeper who had barely broken into a sweat all night he had no problem producing his pots of pee and quickly returned to join up with the other England players. Pearce's urine was less forthcoming. 'You were probably losing 7 or 8 pounds a match through sweat, it was that hot,' he recalls. Pearce drank 14 pints of water in order to try and produce something for the medical officials.

It was while he was sitting in one of the rooms in the cavernous area beneath the stands in the Stadio Delle Alpi that Pearce, his belly swollen with a bucket of water, had an enlightening moment. He was sitting next to the two Germans who had been chosen for the tests and neither of them said a word the whole time they waited. The pair were obviously cock-a-hoop after reaching the final of the World Cup, but out of respect for Pearce in his despair they simply nodded to him and then said nothing. Berthold was one of them, but Pearce cannot remember the other because he was sitting there in despair with his head slumped forward, staring at the floor, in a world of his own. 'The Germans I sat with were so humble. They sat there in total silence, respectful. I don't know if the English would have been like that,' he admits. 'It taught me a bit of a lesson, to be honest.'

Pearce was last on to the team bus, and he wept all the way back to the team hotel while Liz and his parents returned to theirs. The England players congregated in the bar and got drunk, but Pearce peeled off to bed in the room he was sharing with his Forest team-mate Des Walker. By now the water had worked its way through his dehydrated body and after four or five trips to the bathroom he put a bucket next to his bed and each time he felt the urge to go he just rolled onto his side and took aim (with, he insists, more accuracy than he had shown at the penalty spot a few hours earlier).

The England squad returned to a heroes' welcome at Luton airport the next day. Tens of thousands of people lined the streets and cheered the losing semi-finalists who crawled through the town on an open-top bus, taking four hours to go five miles. You'd have thought England had beaten Brazil 5-0 in the final. Like the other players, Pearce was astonished by the warmth of that reception, and relieved that he and Chris Waddle weren't strung up to the first lamp-post by a bloodthirsty mob. But he was embarrassed too, and although he smiled and waved to the crowd, he was feeling awful. He knew that this should have been a victory parade, not a national pat on the back for gallant losers. Pearce may have been the only man in the crowd that day who thought it, but as far as he was concerned it was entirely his fault that England had failed to pull off the country's greatest sporting achievement for twenty-four years.

'I have to admit that Chris and I were relieved that there wasn't a lynch mob waiting for us at Luton,' says Pearce. 'The reception was unbelievable, but to be honest I just wanted to get in the car, go home and see Liz. It was my worst nightmare.' At least Pearce was able to get off that bus smug in the knowledge that, unlike Gazza, he hadn't felt moved to don a pair of plastic breasts. But that was his only consolation.

In the weeks that followed, Pearce received hundreds of letters of support from England fans. There was not a single one blaming him for England's exit, not even from a Derby County fan. Pearce replied to every single letter, touched by the depth of good feeling towards him. Given the partisan nature of English football clubs, this flood of goodwill tells you everything you need to know about Pearce's status amongst English football's followers.

Pearce wanted to throw himself back into football as soon as possible, to immerse himself in his job, blot out the memory of Italia '90 and prove, as if proof were needed, that he was still a great footballer. He didn't have to wait long. After just eight days at home with Liz and their horses, Pearce was back in pre-season training with Nottingham Forest. He played the best football of his life in the 1990/91 campaign, helping Forest to finish eighth in the table and scoring eleven goals along the way. 'I had my best season ever,' says Pearce, simply. For the most part, fans up and down the country declined to taunt him over his penalty miss. Only at Chelsea and Forest's bitter rivals Derby County did he get an earful: 'Pearce is a German! La, la, la, la.' But most left him in peace. (Eight years later, David Beckham, yet to become the nation's darling, suffered a horrible nationwide campaign of vilification after being sent off in England's exit at the hands of Argentina. They even burned his effigy in the East End of London, where he grew up.)

At the European Championships in Sweden in 1992, Pearce was involved in an incident that underlined his reputation not just as a hard man but as a man of enormous self-control. In one of the two memorable episodes in a dour goalless draw with France, Pearce was headbutted by Basile Boli in the area after a French corner. Pearce had jostled with Jocelyn Angloma ('I did leave a little on him,' Pearce confesses) but it was no more than a commonplace bit of pushing and shoving at a set-piece. After England cleared the ball and attention turned upfield, Boli sprinted across the box and ran his head through Pearce's face before continuing his sprint as far from the famous Psycho as possible.

It was a brutal blow and a cowardly act by Boli. Most players would have stayed down – a bit of drama would have attracted the television close-ups and almost certainly led to Boli being suspended for several matches. Others, in their fury and outrage, might have chased Boli up the pitch and had it out with him there and then. Try imagining Vinnie Jones or Roy Keane gingerly trotting back into position and getting on with the game after a headbutt. Pearce, though, immediately picked himself off the turf, shook his head vigorously and walked away. Within minutes the right-hand side of his face had swollen up beneath the large gash under his eye. 'It was something the referee or the linesmen didn't see. But it gave me the hump, as you can imagine,' says Pearce, in a remarkable understatement.

Pat Nevin, watching the match back in Britain, said he was appalled by Boli's assault, but not in the least surprised by the Englishman's reaction. 'Instead of chasing Boli up the line, Stuart did exactly what I would have expected of him,' says Nevin.

Pearce knew that if he floored Boli, he would have been sent off, England would have been down to ten men, exposed at the back and all but out of the competition if defeated. 'This for me is why the name Psycho doesn't hold up,' says Nevin. 'The man is totally controlled.' Far from flying into a fit of rage, he became even more focused, outwardly unmoved by the shock of the incident but inwardly channelling the flood of aggression surging around him into furthering England's cause. He decided to take it out on the innocent Angloma.

'I was not in close quarters with Boli, who was playing at the other end of the pitch,' explains Pearce. 'I was against Angloma, an out-and-out winger, and I still had a job to do with him.' Pearce pointed to his face and said to the knee-knocking Frenchman: 'You've done that and I'm going to sort you out.' Angloma had just had the fear of Pearce put into him. 'Non, non, non, it was not me, it was not me,' he pleaded. Angloma had a quiet end to the game.

Pearce, however, was involved in the only other incident of any significance in the match. England had won a free kick 25 yards out, just to the right of the centre of the goal – his favourite position. There was only one person who was going to take that free kick and Pearce grabbed the ball and set himself up. But as the blood continued to pour from his face, the referee ran over and told him to get off the pitch and get himself cleaned up and treated.

'Don't take this until I get back,' Pearce barked at his team-mates before jogging to the touchline, where his face was cleaned with a towel and Vaseline applied to stop the bleeding. Pearce ran back and as he readied himself to take the kick, Gary Lineker came over and offered the fullback probably the most useless piece of advice he's ever received. 'Just f**king smash it,' said England's captain. The kick, when it finally came, was as predictable as it was ferocious. Rarely can a football have been kicked so hard or a crossbar made to shudder so. The ball crashed against the underside of the woodwork and ricocheted to the ground before being cleared. There was half an inch, perhaps less, between a goal, almost certain victory and quali-fication to the next stage. Just as he had been two years ago in Turin, Pearce was a fraction away from sealing English glory.

At the press conference afterwards, Pearce had the chance to eat his revenge cold. Reporters were eager to ask him about the Boli inci-dent, presuming he would land the Frenchman in 'la merde'. It had been blindingly obvious to all who saw it that Boli's brutal assault was a calculated act. Confirmation from Pearce would have condemned him for the rest of the tournament, perhaps longer. But Pearce, his face still bloated and raw, brushed off the attack as 'an accidental clash of heads', thereby getting Boli and the French off the hook. Rarely in football can one professional have shown such kindness and restraint to an opponent who so palpably did not deserve his forgive-ness. In that one episode, Peace had shown all the qualities that made him a great player of his generation: his hardness, his self-control and his professionalism. 'To be fair to him, Boli was going to help out his team-mate. I would have done exactly the same,' says Pearce, magnanimously. Boli, staggered by the Englishman's generosity, returned to France's team hotel and immediately faxed a letter of thanks to him.

Pearce's international future was cast into doubt following England's failure to qualify for the 1994 World Cup in the United States and the subsequent sacking of manager Graham Taylor. Terry Venables took over, looking for some fresh blood to reinvigorate a side that had looked jaded, one-dimensional and a little confused under the previous regime. Pearce was facing the axe and Venables called to tell him as much. 'I telephoned Stuart and told him that Graeme Le Saux was in my plans and I wanted to take a look at him.' The coded message was not difficult to decipher. It was football-speak for, 'You're in the international wilderness as far as I'm concerned, so if I were you I'd do the decent thing and announce your retirement from the England scene.' Pearce's reaction took Venables aback. He said he understood perfectly and accepted that he would just have to fight for his place. Pearce wasn't going to go away, whether the new manager liked it or not. Once again, the Terminator picked himself up after this latest attempt on him and simply carried on as before. Le Saux, more an attacking wingback than a traditional hard-tackling fullback, suited Venables's tactical readjustments, but Pearce waited patiently in his shadow. He was rewarded before Euro '96 when an injury to Le Saux ruled him out of the biggest sporting event on British soil for thirty years. Pearce, the forgotten man of international football, was back in contention.

He was desperate to play against Scotland, the team he enjoyed seeing England beat more than any other, and he was granted his wish. Pearce was pumped and primed for the occasion at a packed, deafening, colour-filled Wembley. He played against most of the Scottish players at club level and he was friends with some of them, but in the tunnel beforehand they may as well have been suicide bombers for all the bonhomie and warmth he extended them.

'I didn't look at 'em. I didn't shake their hands. Even if I knew them well. After the game it would be different, but this was not the time to be pleasant,' he explains. 'It's a similar thing with boxers. They don't stand around before a fight asking after each other's kids and then go straight into the ring and start hitting lumps out of each other.'

With the game deadlocked at half-time, Venables decided to sacrifice Pearce to bring on Jamie Redknapp to bolster the midfield and give England a more attacking edge. The ploy was a masterstroke, as England swept to a 2-0 victory, sealed with a goal of outrageous impudence by Gascoigne, from a pass laid on by Redknapp. Pearce had no complaints about being substituted. 'As far as I was concerned it was the right thing to do. All I cared about was England beating the Jocks and making sure they had a miserable trip home.'

Already assured of a place in the last sixteen, England annihilated Holland 4-1 in their final group game with one of their most compelling performances in the modern era. Pearce played a full part in the rout and enjoyed rubbing the Dutchmen's noses in it. As wave after wave of England attacks crashed upon the Dutch goal, Jordi Cruyff turned to Pearce and said: 'I don't believe this. What is going on?' To which Pearce replied: 'You f**king better believe it, because it's happening.'

In England's quarter-final against Spain, Pearce's worst nightmare returned to haunt him – the penalty shoot-out. Locked 0-0 after extra time in a match dominated by the Spanish, England – and Pearce – once again found their fate resting on the nerve-wracking lottery of spot kicks. 'I thought it was very selfish of Stuart to put me through that again,' says Liz, wryly.

Venables came onto the pitch to sort out his order of takers, when Pearce marched up to him and said 'I want to take one.'

'Are you sure?' said Venables, a little incredulous.

'Too right I'm sure.'

Pearce had been to hell and back and now he wanted to make another visit. England fans inside Wembley and watching on television looked at each other nervously as Pearce, head down and thighs pumping, strode out of the centre circle and into the Spanish penalty box to place his ball on the spot.

'The pressure on myself was ridiculous,' says Psycho. The nation held its breath as Pearce made his run-up before unleashing a net-buster into the corner of the net. The Spanish goalkeeper had dived the right way, but there was no way he was stopping Pearce's thunderbolt. Pearce's reaction has become one of the most enduring football images of the period. Bellowing like a sergeant-major at raw recruits on the parade ground, veins and muscles bursting out of his neck, his eyes popping out of their sockets, Pearce punched the air in the direction of England's deliriously relieved fans. Had he just been spared the electric chair with a minute to go and told he had also won the National Lottery jackpot, it is difficult to imagine him expressing more forcefully his relief and joy at burying that penalty. You only have to imagine how he might have felt had he missed in order to appreciate the immense courage it took to volunteer for football's equivalent of a jog through 'sniper valley'. Pearce would have turned to stone with shame.

'Even when I see it now I still laugh – in relief with Stuart,' says Venables. England won the match – the only time of the four occasions in their history that they have emerged victorious from a penalty shoot-out – after Nadal saw his effort saved by Seaman. Pearce immediately sought out the wayward Spanish penalty taker to offer his condolences.

For Pearce the match was a personal triumph as well as a national one. The World Cup miss would haunt him forever, but he had at least proved to himself and the public that he could face his demons.

But the football Furies would not let him rest. There was still one more challenge for him to face. Four days later he was once again called upon to make that long walk upfield to the penalty spot, when England's semi-final against Germany was left without a winner after extra time. The bloody Germans again – with a place in the final at stake, just as there had been six years previously. In another parallel with Italia '90, the winners of this penalty shoot-out would be favourites to take the title against a theoretically weaker side in the final, in this instance, the Czech Republic, the dark horses of Euro '96. If Pearce missed his penalty on this occasion his heroic courage against Spain would have counted for nothing. He would forever be remembered as the player who, not once but twice, 'bottled' it against the Germans with a place in the final of a major tournament at stake. He was feeling bad enough after his rare defensive lapse had allowed Stefan Kuntz to equalize for the Germans. Whereas he had waited quietly and nervously in the centre circle for his turn against Spain, now he was marching amongst his colleagues, his eyes bulging, tapping his head and calling on his team-mates to cast aside any doubts in their mind.

When his number was up with the two teams locked at 2-2, he strode purposefully towards the goal area, laid his ball on the spot, turned and fired his shot to his right as Andreas Kopke dived the other way. 'I found it funny that Barry Davies described it as a brilliant penalty on the television,' he says now, 'because as far as I was concerned it was a pile of shite. The goalkeeper had simply gone the wrong way.'

The teams were level at 5-5 as the shoot-out headed into sudden death. Pearce had done his bit and now he could only stand and watch as Gareth Southgate, England's sixth penalty taker, headed towards football's equivalent of the gallows hoping for a last-minute pardon. Southgate had only taken one penalty in professional football – which he had missed – and as every England fan recalls with a shudder of despair, he failed once again as his weak shot was comfortably saved by Kopke. Andreas Moller, by contrast, nervelessly dispatched his penalty into the top corner with David Seaman floundering on the turf across the other side of the goal. Germany were through to the final and once again England's players left the field in misery. Pearce, mindful of his own feelings of desolation at Italia '90, was among the first to seek out Southgate to comfort him.

• • •

Stuart Pearce announced his retirement from international football on the team bus after the Germany match, but before putting down his microphone he told his captive audience that he would still be around the club scene 'to kick s**t out of them on Saturdays'. As it turned out, Pearce was twice called out of retirement by England's two subsequent managers, Glenn Hoddle and Kevin Keegan. He was not much more than a stopgap on each occasion, but he acquitted himself as admirably as anyone could have expected of a man heading into his late thirties. Nor was his club career drawing to a close. After Forest, he headed north to Newcastle, where he somehow managed to keep his dignity despite the humiliations heaped on him during the controversial, if brief, managership of Ruud Gullit, the unhappiest time of Pearce's career. (Pearce probably didn't help his cause by dumping the manager on his backside at every available opportunity in training.)

Pearce's legend as a man of granite was already set in stone when he was involved in a horrifying accident in 1997 that served only to compound his reputation for indestructibility. It happened when Pearce was left at home nursing a minor injury while Newcastle set off on a pre-season tour. He had just left his house to go to a meeting when a dustcart came careering around the corner, hit the kerb, flipped over and landed on top of his car. In the split second before impact, Pearce doubtless thought he was about to die, but had enough presence of mind to throw himself horizontally across the passenger seat. The dustcart crashed down, crushing the car, but Pearce was left unscathed. Had he remained sitting upright he would have certainly died, but there was a small space left between him and the collapsed roof. The heavily shaken driver of the dustcart came round and smashed the window, allowing Pearce to climb through. Pearce was not happy and immediately flew into a rage, first at the driver of the dustcart and then at another driver who stopped at the scene. (Your heart goes out to Pearce, but also to the dustcart driver, who, moments after surviving a horrifying accident, was suddenly confronted by Stuart Pearce in an extremely bad mood. It's difficult to say which would be more frightening.) Pearce had suffered nothing worse than a nick to the skin as he squeezed through the shattered window, and people up and down the country were left wondering if there was anything, on or off a football pitch, that could stop the man.

Harry Redknapp rescued him from his hell in the north-east and took him to West Ham. Pearce rewarded Redknapp's faith with a good season for the East London club – good enough for the fans to vote him

Player of the Season. Two broken legs in quick succession appeared to have signalled the end for Pearce, but once again he showed his Terminator-like qualities and returned to action. Most players would have accepted defeat at the age of thirty-nine and opened a pub, or applied for a post as youth team coach at a former club. But Pearce was having none of it and battled back to full fitness which, once achieved, led to Keegan bringing him to Manchester City to help their push for promotion back to the top flight. Ever the pragmatist, however, Pearce used the time off during his isolation at Newcastle and his lay-offs through injury to take some FA coaching courses. When he finally hangs up his boots, Pearce will be perfectly prepared to step into a top coaching role: young enough to relate to the players, yet experienced and qualified to guarantee their respect as a coach. Even before retiring as a player, Pearce had already gained experience as a manager when he took over after Frank Clark, Clough's successor, parted company with Forest. He was even named Manager of the Month there for his first four weeks in charge.

More than any other player of his generation, Stuart Pearce MBE represents the true spirit of England, as perceived by the majority of fans who travel the world in support of the national team: a man who lives as far away from the world of celebrity as his fame and popularity will allow. A man who has never dived to win a penalty or free kick; raw, unfashionably patriotic, calm in a crisis, uncomplaining, totally dedicated to the cause, pragmatic not pretty, a Tommy Atkins trench fighter. And an Englishman to the tips of his boots.

BRIAN CLOUGH
THE MAN WHO WALKED ON THE TRENT

It was towards the end of the 1992/93 season and Brian Clough stood at the side of the pitch at the City Ground, tears running down his cheeks. Most football managers would have been booed out of the ground after their team had been relegated. But as Clough shivered and twitched with emotion, the visiting Sheffield United fans began to chant his name. The crowd then rose as one and sang his praises until their tonsils practically burst: 'Brian Clough is a football genius, Brian Clough is a football genius, Brian Clough is a football genius...'

• • •

It is difficult to know where to begin when discussing the life and character of such a colourful, complex man. Even Clough himself, someone with a forceful opinion on everything, would struggle to tell you what he was all about.

His personality dominated English football management for more than two decades, even when his teams were being overshadowed by rivals. To some he was a rude, arrogant tyrant. A number of his players even hid from him in the cupboard or the toilets. ('I would love to be the perfect dictator,' Clough liked to say.) To others, 'the man who walked on the Trent' was a character of great conscience with an old-fashioned, noble view of how football should be played and of how his players should conduct themselves on and off the pitch. Former Labour leader Michael Foot described him as 'one of the best social- ists I have ever known'. To David Pleat he is simply 'the most amaz- ing man I've ever met'.

No one knew where they stood with Brian Clough. He could behave like a doting father but the very next minute deliver a withering putdown. A man of multiple contradictions, Clough was a strict disci- plinarian but was happy to take his players on a drinking binge the night before a European Cup final. He read *The Guardian* but wrote for *The Sun* and other tabloids, and earned a good living outside football by writing for the press but loved ridiculing journalists, turning off their dictaphones at the start of an interview or screwing up the question sheets of a young reporter before going live on air. Former England defender Stuart Pearce, his long-serving captain at Nottingham Forest, said that the only predictable thing about Clough was his unpredictabil- ity. But even Pearce, a man of fierce loyalty and tough moral fibre, grew tired of Clough's exasperatingly erratic behaviour and stubborn manner towards the end of their working relationship.

Whether they loved him or loathed him, all Clough's players (with the exception of some at Leeds United) would acknowledge his remarkable powers as a football manager. His greatest triumphs came at Derby County and Nottingham Forest, two medium-sized, 'unfashionable' clubs with modest followings. Working with limited budgets, Clough transformed both teams from Second Division workhorses into thoroughbred English champions, playing slick passing football. Clough could be tactically cute when the match demanded it, but he believed in giving the paying public their money's worth and in putting on a show. 'If God wanted football played in the air, why did he put grass on the ground?' was a typical Clough training-ground mantra.

• • •

Brian Clough was born and brought up in Middlesborough, a goal kick's distance from Ayresome Park, the football ground where he would shoot to national prominence as a teenager. He was one of the finest strikers of his day, first with Middlesborough and then north-east rivals Sunderland, reaching 250 goals more quickly than anyone else in English football history. Clough only played twice for England, despite a vociferous campaign for him to be given a regular place. The fact that all but one of his goals came in the Second Division did not help his cause, while the prolific form of Tottenham's Jimmy Greaves also restricted his chances. In six seasons with Middlesborough, Clough scored 204 goals in 222 appearances and was the country's leading goal scorer in the 1958/59 campaign.

But even this early in his footballing career, Brian Clough's personality was making itself felt. As a young player, Clough showed his capacity for stirring up trouble and resentment, and such was his unpop-ularity in the changing room that his Middlesborough team-mates campaigned – successfully – to have him removed as captain. He was said to have been so selfish as a player that he would push his team-mates off the ball, and although that's probably an exaggeration, like all great strikers he certainly preferred to keep the ball rather than pass it when he was in sight of goal. Clough joined Sunderland in 1961, where his remarkable goal scoring continued and he found the net sixty-three times in seventy-four appearances for the Wearside club.

Clough's playing career was wrecked in a split-second on Boxing Day 1962, when he tore the cruciate ligament in his knee in an FA Cup game against Bury. He was only twenty-nine at the time and he battled frantically to salvage his career, putting himself through a punishing rehabilitation schedule, but all to no avail. After a whole season on the sidelines he did manage a return to action at the start of the next, but he played only a handful of games before having to accept that he was permanently crocked.

Almost immediately, Clough launched himself into a coaching career. He was put in charge of the Sunderland youth team and quickly showed his gift for bringing the best out of players. The club manager at Sunderland was Alan Brown, a domineering but fair-minded disciplinarian who had made a major impression on the ambitious young Clough. Brown was a man who inspired fear and awe in his players, just as Clough would throughout his managerial career.

In October 1965, thirty-five-year-old Clough became the youngest manager in the Football League when he accepted an offer to manage Hartlepool United, then languishing at the foot of the Fourth Division. He duly set about transforming one of the poorest professional clubs in England into promotion contenders within a year. His first move was to bring in his old friend Peter Taylor, and so began the most successful double act in the history of football management.

Clough's boyish looks were not the only quality that made him stand out from the sheepskins of the managerial crowd. His obvious flair for management was matched by his eccentricity and his gift for self-publicity. Clough grabbed headlines when he decided to qualify as a bus driver so that he could drive the team coach and save the club some money. He showed from the earliest days of his managerial career that he knew how to work the media to his own advantage: give them a story and they will give you a platform for self-promotion. Clough made sure he had several journalists in tow when he toured around Hartlepool, driving from pub to pub and working men's clubs to drum up support for his team. Within months Hartlepool United – and in particular its oddball, bombastic manager – were attracting a level of media attention out of all proportion to their status.

It was at Hartlepool that Clough battled his first chairman, and developed a taste for directors' blood. Chairman Ernie Ord, whom Clough later described as one of the most evil men he had ever met, tried to sack his partner Taylor; when Clough stood up to him, Ord tried to sack him too. Clough simply refused to go and after a hastily convened board meeting it was Ord, not the cocksure young manager, who cleared his desk.

Clough left Hartlepool for greater things in the summer of 1967, leaving behind a team transformed from moribund no-hopers into one of the best in the division. Impressed by Clough's magical makeover at Hartlepool, Derby County lured him to the Second Division in the hope that he could work similar miracles. There was nothing remarkable about Derby – like most professional football clubs, they were special only to those who followed them. They had won the FA Cup in 1946, a time when the professional game was struggling to find its feet again after the disruptions of a world war. They had also won the Third Division North title. But that was it.

Derby would not be disappointed by their investment in Clough and Taylor. Within two years, the Rams were in the top flight and within another three they were crowned league champions. The Derby players did not have to wait long after Clough's arrival to discover that powerful winds of change were about to sweep through the peeling corridors underneath the Baseball Ground. Stopping just short of kicking down the dressing room door and pulling two pistols from a holster, Clough met the Derby players for the first time and told them they had three weeks to impress him or they would be out on their ears. Not many did impress him, and a major clear out of the club from top to bottom was soon in full swing. Even two tea ladies were swept out when they were heard giggling after a home defeat.

It was Taylor, though, not Clough, who had the eye for promising players. Taylor would bring the player in and Clough would mould – or bully – the best out of him. Clough joked later that if a player turned out to be good, then he would tell everyone he was one of his signings, but if the player flopped, then he was one of Taylor's or Ronnie Fenton's (another assistant at Forest). In those early years at Derby, Clough and Taylor brought in and developed several players who went on to greater things. One of them was defender Roy McFarland, then at Tranmere, who would play twenty-eight times for England. His signing for Derby was a classic piece of Clough-and-Taylor showmanship. The pair travelled up to Merseyside, knocked on the door of the McFarland family home in the small hours and got his parents to get the youngster out of bed. Within half an hour a bleary-eyed McFarland had signed forms and was tucked up again, while Derby's Dynamic Duo were disappearing back down the motorway.

Clough would try any trick to get his man. At one point he was eager to sign Scotland midfielder Archie Gemmill, but was aware that Gemmill's wife did not think the world of him. So, he turned up at their home, washed the dishes and generally charmed the apron off Mrs Gemmill until she finally came round to the idea of her husband joining Derby.

Players who worked under Clough say he was a ruthless man who would stop at nothing to see his will done. However, many also recall how tender-hearted he could be, often helping out players' families who were tight for money or having flowers sent to a family home in difficult times.

Clough brought unimaginable success to the sleepy Midlands club. After winning the Second Division title in 1969, they finished fourth in the First Division the following season. Two years later they were crowned champions – albeit by a mathematical whisker – pipping Leeds and Liverpool, who both failed to win their final games of the season. Derby were now a major force in European football and the following year they reached the semi-finals of the European Cup. They were denied a place in the final when they lost 3-1 on aggregate to Juventus in a match that newspapers claimed was rigged in the Italians' favour. Clough gave his opponents a blast of blunt northern invective after the first leg in Turin, calling the hosts 'f**king cheating Italian bastards' in the press conference. For good measure, he then went on to question their courage in the war.

Back in England, another kind of confrontation was brewing between Clough and Sam Longson, Derby's chairman. Longson and his directors didn't like the way Clough threw his weight about, or his habit of arranging the transfer of a new player and only telling the board about it when he put the bill on the table after the deal was done. In one of the bitterest feuds between chairman and manager in the history of the English game, the players sided with their manager and threatened to follow him out of the club if he was forced to go. Clough finally resigned in October 1973, eighteen months after the row first blew up, but as a final two-fingered salute, he turned up at the Baseball Ground for their first home match after his departure and sat himself a few yards away from the directors, basking in the hero's reception the fans gave him.

The following year would be the lowest point in a managerial career spanning four decades. Tempted by a good contract and the flexibility of the easy-going chairman Mike Bamber, Clough and Taylor joined Brighton in the Third Division. But it was clear from the outset that Clough's heart was not in it and he spent a lot of time away from the Goldstone Ground. He was constantly travelling back up to his east Midlands home or disappearing on trips abroad. He had only been there for eight months when the departure of Don Revie from Leeds United to take over as England manager was to catapult Clough back into the limelight in one of the most bizarre episodes in English football history.

Many observers thought that appointing the country's most abrasive, headstrong manager to take charge of the country's most abrasive, headstrong team would only end in tears. And it took just forty-four days to prove them right. The fact that Clough had spent the last five years calling Leeds 'dirty cheats' was always going to hamper dressing room harmony. He had even suggested on television that the Yorkshire club should have been demoted to the Second Division for their disciplinary record. What's more, Leeds had dominated English football since the end of the 1960s, and their team of ageing veterans were never likely to be receptive to a new master trying to teach them new tricks. But the Leeds board wanted a man strong enough to deal with a team of established stars, a man unlikely to be fazed by living in the shadow of Don Revie, by some distance the club's greatest manager. The working relationship between the country's most feared team and its most feared manager was a total disaster. 'It was a marriage made in hell,' sums up former Leeds winger Duncan McKenzie.

The new era at the club didn't get off to a great start when Clough, having signed a highly lucrative contract, hopped on a flight to Majorca for a holiday. When he finally appeared back in Leeds, he turned up very late for the club's traditional pre-season get-together with players, wives and back-up staff. Leeds had become a tight family under Revie; the new father figure was already behaving like a runaway.

Leeds' forward Peter Lorimer recalls Clough's brief tenure vividly. 'Everyone at Leeds was shocked when they heard Clough was coming. If there was one manager in the country they didn't want, it was him.' Clough made no attempt to hide his enduring contempt for his predecessor Revie, a god-like figure at Elland Road. 'The first thing he did was to ask for all the furniture in his office to be taken away,' says Lorimer. 'He wouldn't sit on the same seat as Don Revie, and we realized he really hated Don and the Leeds set-up.'

Norman Hunter is another Leeds player who has nothing but bad memories of Clough's reign. 'For the first two or three days' training, we didn't see him. We didn't know what was happening.' When Clough finally entered the Leeds dressing room, what he said to the players killed off any possibility of a working relationship before it had even started. 'At the team meeting he said that he wanted to make his impressions first,' Hunter recalls, 'and then he said, "Before I start working with you I want to tell you what I think of you lot," and he then launched an attack on every player.'

Clough accused the Leeds team of being cheats, and told them their achievements meant nothing because they hadn't played the game fairly. 'I said we'll have to cut out this harassing of referees, because Leeds had perfected it,' recalls Clough. 'Whenever there was a free kick you could never see the referee because he was always surrounded by white shirts, protesting, shoving and barging. It was cheating.'

Lorimer recalls the mounting amazement at Clough's tirade. 'His finishing gambit was: "You've won all the trophies, but as far as I'm concerned you can throw all your medals in the bin because you've not won anything fairly."' And as Norman Hunter points out: 'That was not the thing to say to fifteen or sixteen internationals.'

Clough hadn't 'lost' the dressing room – he had never come close to winning them over in the first place. From then on, it was obvious to all concerned that he wouldn't be able to manage the way he wanted to. Some feel that had Peter Taylor been there at Clough's side to act as a buffer between him and the players, the Leeds episode may have had a very different ending. 'If Peter Taylor wasn't going with him, he shouldn't have gone, because Peter would have told him who to look out for,' says the *Sun*'s John Sadler, who ghosted Clough's autobiography.

John O'Hare, one of the players Clough brought in on his arrival, explains that his new team-mates were dumbfounded by the manager's behaviour. 'The players just couldn't accept that he was a good manager. They were asking me: "Was he like this at Derby?"'

Six games into the new season, the off-pitch tensions had clearly communicated themselves to the team on the pitch. Leeds had won just one game and a crisis club meeting was called. Clough was given a light grilling by the Leeds board, who asked him what was going on. 'I said just give it a bit longer,' Clough recalls, 'but I twigged he'd made his mind up. I tried to do things too quickly. Right or wrong, I did it.' The players were asked for their opinions, and Clough's fate was sealed. 'We just told them that Clough doesn't like Leeds United, he doesn't like the players and he had insulted all of us,' recalls Lorimer.

Clough's forty-four days at Leeds offers one of the best opportunities for a piece of 'What if ...?' speculation in English football. Leeds went rapidly downhill in the mid-1970s and it wasn't until the early 1990s that they re-established themselves among the footballing elite. Clough, meanwhile, would go on to produce one of the most remarkable success stories in European football history with Nottingham Forest. If he had handled those first few days at Leeds with more tact, if he had won the respect of his players, then one can only wonder at what he and the best club in the country at the time might have achieved. That said, Clough didn't seem too upset when he appeared outside Elland Road with Leeds officials to announce his departure in September 1974, just a few weeks into the new season. In fact, he was smiling from ear to ear. He had persuaded the Leeds board to pay up the full £100,000 due to him for a four-year contract.

• • •

Clough had reached the nadir of his managerial career. At first, there were fears that other top clubs wouldn't be interested in him after the failures at Leeds and Brighton. There were some compensating factors, though, as he explains: 'I said to the wife: "I've got a house in Leeds, a house in Brighton and a house in Derby. What am I, a football manager or a property developer?"'

As it turned out, Brian Clough was not long in the managerial wilderness. Four months after leaving Leeds he was back in the dugout, this time as manager at the City Ground, home of Nottingham Forest. Forest, like Derby, were a middle-ranking club with a modest history, an average gate of 11,000 and a position in the lower half of the Second Division. In the 1975/76 campaign, Clough's first full season at the club, they finished eighth in the table but it wasn't until he persuaded his old sidekick Peter Taylor to leave Brighton and join him in his new venture that the club truly began to go places. The brotherly affection between Clough and Taylor was to become even stronger over the next seven years or so, as football's top double act put on a show that had Forest fans pinching themselves in disbelief. 'We thought that together we would have success quicker than if we did it individually,' Taylor reflected shortly before his death, in a breathtaking understatement on the effectiveness of their partnership.

At the end of 1976/77 Forest won promotion to the First Division and by Christmas they were top of the table. Clough chose the time to put himself forward as a candidate to succeed Revie as England manager. Clough's predecessor at Leeds had left the England post in disgrace after walking out mid-contract, and in the middle of the country's World Cup qualifying campaign, having been seduced by a huge cash offer to manage the United Arab Emirates. Clough thought he was the ideal man to fill the vacant post, and he told the FA as much. 'I had a magnificent interview,' he told the media modestly, after leaving Lancaster Gate. The FA and its patrician chairman Sir Harold Thompson were not so sure. Clough was the overwhelming people's favourite for the job, but it eventually went to former West Ham manager Ron Greenwood, a quiet, thoughtful figure unlikely to start throwing the crockery around inside Lancaster Gate. 'They were scared stiff of him,' says former Forest striker Gary Birtles.

'I took it as an insult that somebody who knew nothing about football was in charge of the interview,' Clough later commented, scornfully. Today, he is still upset that he was passed over for the job by people he had no respect for. 'They gave it to Ron Greenwood – a typical Football Association decision,' he says. 'Ron is a charming man who wouldn't hurt a fly and couldn't fall out with his wife if he tried. They just didn't want any trouble.' But in the same breath, he admits, 'They were shrewd, because they were thinking I was going to take over the FA. And they were right – I was going to take over the FA lock, stock and barrel.'

Clough wasted no time in showing the FA the managerial qualities they had turned down. Forest finished the season as champions and League Cup winners in their first year after promotion. At the time, only one other manager had won the championship with different clubs – Herbert Chapman with Huddersfield and Arsenal in the 1920s and 1930s. (Kenny Dalglish would later become the third, with success at Liverpool and then Blackburn.) Clough – with the help of Taylor's eye for a good player – had built a formidable team in less than two years. From the second half of the 1977/78 season to halfway through the next, Clough's side went unbeaten in forty-two league games and in a total of eighty-four league matches over those two seasons, they lost just six times. Rarely can a team of such force and style have been welded together so quickly.

Clough's great skill was to get the absolute maximum out of his players, both as a team and as individuals, turning average players into very good ones. Winger John Robertson, midfielders Martin O'Neill and John McGovern, strikers Gary Birtles, Tony Woodcock and Kenny Burns and defender Viv Anderson all benefited from Clough's magical touch and fearful inspiration. In striker Trevor Francis, Scotland midfielder Archie Gemmill, goalkeeper Peter Shilton and central defender Larry Lloyd, Clough also had some players of outstanding natural ability who needed little polishing. Former Liverpool defender Lloyd admits that the exasperatingly provocative manager lifted his game to new heights. Lloyd was the victim of one of Clough's stock psychological tricks – to abuse and humiliate a player into proving the criticism was wrong. One of the most rugged defenders in the league, Lloyd was once called a coward by Clough after missing a tackle. He was furious and Clough got the response from him he wanted – in the matches that followed, Lloyd threw himself into the fray with even greater aggression and determination than normal. At the end of his career, Lloyd called Clough the best manager he had ever played for – and that included the Liverpool greats Bill Shankley and Bob Paisley: 'I didn't like him as a man and I used to row with him a lot, but he was an unbeliev-able manager.'

Another player to benefit from Clough's ruthlessness was Kenny Burns, a run-of-the-mill defender whom Clough converted into a top striker. Burns, no delicate flower himself, once found himself being shoved against the wall by Clough, who told him that he would throw him straight back into non-league football if he ever had any trouble from him. And Clough had no hesitation in selling very good players if he didn't like them, as John Sheridan and Gary Megson could testify after they were dumped onto the transfer market in the 1980s with no explanation.

Clough's ruthlessness and off-hand manner didn't work with every-one, and some players were put off him from the moment they met. One of them was Gary McAllister, one of the best British midfielders of his generation and a decent, unassuming man. Clough was late for their first meeting and entirely unapologetic when he finally made an appearance. McAllister, a future Scotland captain, decided there and then that he did not want to work for someone who showed such little respect. Stuart Pearce, Clough's long-serving captain in the late 1980s and early 1990s, ended up blanking Clough for most of what turned out to be the manager's final season at the club in 1992/93. Pearce had asked him several times about thrashing out a new contract deal, but Clough failed to turn up for their meetings and ignored Pearce's appeals to discuss his future. For Pearce, Clough's off-hand manner was just plain discourtesy. He had served him as a player for over eight years – and as a captain for almost as long – and he felt deeply upset that his manager could not be bothered to take time to help him sort out his livelihood. When Kingsley Black came up from Luton to discuss a possible move to Forest, Clough made him take off his shoes to see his real height, called him a coward, then made him hand over his watch, saying he would only give it back to him if he came back the following day and signed for him.

Clough was generally careful with the club's money when it came to transfers and he preferred not to buy a player than to risk a bad investment. But in yet another paradox, he also became the first manager to spend £1 million on a player, when he bought Trevor Francis from Birmingham. Francis was quickly made aware that he would not be receiving special treatment at Forest. His first game for his new club was for the reserves in front of twenty-five spectators, and after the match Clough humiliated him in the dressing room, shouting at him for attempting a bicycle kick during the match.

Clough's training ground regime was extremely unpredictable. His teams often began the season slowly because the players were often far less fit than their rivals and it was only through playing matches that they became properly fit. Occasionally, Clough would pack up a practice session barely fifteen minutes after it had started if he wasn't in the mood for it. A typical Clough training session involved six-a-side matches between the players with him on the sidelines, in his trade-mark green sweatshirt, waving a stick and shouting abuse at wrong-doers. On one occasion, apparently bored by what he was watching, Clough made the entire squad run through a giant patch of nettles.

Brian Clough was an outstanding galvanizer of men and a shrewd tactician, but he had little or no interest in preparation. While other managers drilled their teams like sergeant majors on the parade ground, Clough would often be looking for ways to amuse and divert himself. Once asked what he believed the secret of great coaching to be, he replied: 'I'll tell you what coaching is – telling McFarland to get his bloody hair cut.' (Short haircuts were one of his enduring obsessions.)

Alan Hill, one of the members of the Forest bootroom, says Clough almost delighted in ridiculing those who laid so much store by the importance of coaching. 'Cloughie used to shout: "Coaching? Don't talk to me about coaching. Come with me – I'll show you coaching." And then he would stand there with a stick shouting "Hit the target! Hit the target! HIT THE TARGET!" Now that's coaching.'

Forest players never knew who was meant to be in a defensive wall, or what they were meant to do at free kicks. Clough's team talks were rarely tactical and he was magnificently unconcerned about informing his team about the strengths of the opposition. His players would often go to Clough's backroom staff to try and establish what they were meant to be doing at set-pieces, but most of the time Forest just made it up as they went along. It seems remarkable now, at a time when the ability of coaches is so highly prized, that a man with only a passing interest in tactics and the qualities of the opposition could twice lead a team to European Cup glory.

Clough's greatest quality was his ability to get the best out of his players as characters, not as footballers, whether by fear or by guile. For Clough, football was a simple game and whenever he did hand out specific playing advice it often got straight to the heart of the player's problem. Stuart Pearce recalls how Clough spent an entire training session berating him to stay on his feet. It was only afterwards that the future England fullback realized the importance of Clough's ranting. All his playing career he had been sliding into tackles, but occasionally he would be left sitting on his backside as the winger danced off towards the penalty area. From that moment on, and for the rest of his career, Pearce would try to stay on his feet, shadowing his opponent. By picking up on one basic flaw in Pearce's game, Clough had transformed a good fullback into an England international.

That said, when Pearce was called up to the England squad for the first time, Clough demonstrated his peculiar habit of deflating egos and snubbing players out of the blue. He called Pearce into his office and asked him 'Do you think you're good enough to be an England player?' Pearce answered that he didn't know but would have to find out, to which Clough replied: 'I don't think you are, now get out.'

Clough's eccentricities were a feature of life at Nottingham Forest throughout his tenure. Alan Hill recalls one team talk that Clough gave before a crucial league match which left the squad in a state of bemused confusion. 'Imagine the dressing room full of about fifteen players before kick-off. They are all quiet and ready to hang on his every word. Then he starts singing "Fly Me To the Moon" and after he finishes he says to the players: "You're brilliant players, brilliant, that's why you play for me. Now go out there in front of your grandmas and your grandfathers, your wives, girlfriends and your kids, go out there and make them feel proud. I'm a good singer, but you're good footballers. Now you're going to win today lads, aren't you? Aren't you?"' He would do anything, no matter how unorthodox, to get the best performance out of his players, even administering large glasses of whisky or brandy before they headed off down the tunnel.

Clough ruled Forest like a generally benign crackpot dictator, making decisions on a whim that everyone had to fall in with or risk being alienated or humiliated. He would often announce at one or two days' notice that the team would be flying abroad to play in a friendly in order to earn some extra cash for the club. On the way to a match at Luton, the Forest players found themselves walking up and down the hard shoulder on the M1 for half an hour after Clough ordered the driver to pull over because they were running early. On another occasion, his players were asked to walk a gauntlet of hate among Millwall fans, whose reputation for violence was second to none in the 1980s. In order to show the south London club that his team would not be cowed by intimidation, Clough ordered the driver to park the coach half a mile from the ground and, with him at the head like an all-conquering general, he marched his whole squad through the crowd of bemused Millwall supporters.

Clough's magic invariably rubbed off on his players, who felt strangely lifted by his unconventional approach and his extraordinary powers of motivation. 'He was one of those guys you wanted to run your socks off for,' says John Robertson, the sublimely skilled left-winger who did so much to light up the Clough era.

Forest's dazzling rise from mid-Second Division obscurity took them to the summit of Continental club football when they won the European Cup in 1979 and then retained it the following year. In the 1979 final in Munich, Trevor Francis's goal was enough to beat Swedish club Malmo. Forest, the holders, were drawn against Liverpool, the English champions, in the first round of the following year's competition. On paper Liverpool were the superior side, but Forest won the first leg 2-0 at the City Ground. Sensing anxiety in the camp ahead of the second leg at Anfield, Clough decided to take his own, very curious, assertive action. His plan was simple – he plied his team with booze at lunchtime and then sent them to bed in the afternoon. Fully relaxed, the players kept their composure in the frenzied atmosphere at Anfield that evening, and ground out an impressive goalless draw. Before the

1980 European Cup Final against Hamburg in Madrid, Clough took his players on a holiday to Majorca for a week. There was no training, but drinking and relaxation were encouraged. And Forest beat the Germans 1-0. Afterwards, however, Clough revealed that awkward, unfathomable side of his personality again, when he refused to let his players meet up with their wives and partners to celebrate. The players protested, but Clough refused to yield.

Brian Clough's extraordinary achievements with Forest are matched only by his idiosyncratic approach to match preparation. Can you imagine Arsene Wenger passing the brandy bottle around the Arsenal dressing room before a vital European match? 'We treated Europe as a holiday,' explains Clough. 'The league was our bread and butter – that was hard. But when we used to go abroad, we saw it as a change of air. We never trained for those matches.' Clough's feelings towards our Continental cousins have not mellowed with time. 'I don't like Germans – they shot my father,' he states flatly. 'I don't like the French either. They don't like us and we don't like them and we got them out of the shit in two world wars. I couldn't work with these foreign players like today. They wouldn't understand what I was saying and I certainly don't speak half their languages. But there was one thing they would understand, and that's "f**k off".'

Perhaps surprisingly, given such hard-headedness, Brian Clough nearly became an MP. At one time he was considered as a Labour candidate for one of the wards in Derby. He was an enthusiastic socialist – although his considerable wealth, compared to that of the average worker, and willingness to accept money from right-wing newspapers for a weekly column, hardly sat easily with his political beliefs. He once gave free tickets to 200 striking miners for a Derby game and relished canvassing for a Labour candidate in Derby North, making funny, rabble-rousing speeches and ridiculing politicians. 'We have X number of MPs and if you took a cross-section of the public or a profession, I do not think you would find so many dishonest people per thousand,' he announced during one campaign. Michael Foot referred to Clough in his speeches at the Labour Party Conference. 'What he wanted to see was a decent society and he wanted to use his influence to further it and he was as much interested in that as he was in football matters,' says Foot. 'He was trying to teach a new kind of spirit in the community.' Politics' loss was football's gain.

• • •

Forest's form slumped in the first two seasons of the 1980s as the club off-loaded several of their leading players and failed to bring in quality replacements. At the end of the 1981/82 campaign, in which Forest finished twelfth, Peter Taylor announced his retirement, saying he was unhappy with his recent performance. His departure was a major blow for Clough and Forest. 'I wouldn't say 50 per cent of Clough's effectiveness was lost when Peter Taylor walked out, but it was a big percentage,' says John Sadler. Clough was upset at his departure, although the split seemed amicable enough. 'I didn't want him to retire,' says Clough. 'He used to say to me, "When you get shot of me, there won't be as much laughter in your life." He was right.' Within a few months, however, the two old friends had a very public falling out and never spoke again. Clough was said to have been mildly put out when Taylor took the manager's job at Derby the following season, but it wasn't until Taylor poached Forest winger John Robertson without consulting Clough that a real row erupted. Alan Hill remembers the moment Clough discovered that Robertson was joining Derby. 'When Clough heard, he went and bought a bottle of whisky from the bar, slammed it down on the table and said, "I'll never, ever, ever talk to that man again in my life." And he didn't. Later he said that if Peter Taylor was on fire at the side of the motorway he wouldn't get out of his car to put it out. That's how bitter he was.'

John Sadler thought it regrettable that the two should have fallen out so drastically over such a trivial point. 'For heaven's sake, here they were at loggerheads over what was essentially a football matter – and, moreover, Robertson's best football days were behind him as well. It was never really healed, either, before Peter died.'

Forest's European Cup triumph in 1980 would be the club's last trophy for ten years, but Clough slowly began to rebuild the team. It was often said that Taylor did the buying while Clough did the management. Later in life Clough himself would say that he was 'the shop window' and his assistant was 'the goods in the store'. But with the help of his new assistant Ronnie Fenton, Clough showed he could put together a powerful team without Taylor's input. Forest acquired some top-quality players in Stuart Pearce, Des Walker, Neil Webb, Clough's son Nigel, Steve Hodge, Franz Carr and Roy Keane. In 1988 and 1989 they finished third in the table and won the League Cup in both years. Forest appeared to be on the verge of dominating English football again for a second time under Clough's management.

It was not to be. In October 1990, Peter Taylor died. Clough was devastated and he cut a haunted, tearful figure when he arrived for the funeral in the Nottinghamshire village of Widmerpool. He was later filled with remorse about the feud with the person closest to him outside his immediate family. 'There is no doubt Clough loved Taylor,' says former Forest midfielder Martin O'Neill. Clough even dedicated his autobiography to Taylor, and spoke movingly about his friendship with him in the book. Clough had been no stranger to the bottle up to that point, but after Taylor's death, his drinking became markedly heavier. 'I think that's when the drinking started,' says Alan Hill. 'He liked to drink and at times he drank a little too much. We all did. It became an everyday thing with him and unfortunately it affected Brian more than most, which was sad.'

Clough's behaviour became even more erratic and unpredictable at the start of the new decade. In 1991 he was seen on television punching fans who ran onto the pitch after a League Cup match against QPR. Clough was enraged, commenting that it was like having uninvited guests burst into his kitchen. There were fears that the Football Association might impose a lengthy suspension, but in the end he got away with what most considered to be a lenient punishment of a £5,000 fine and a three-month touchline ban. Clough managed to take some of the sting out of the episode when he appeared before the television cameras at the City ground alongside two of the fans he had punched and got them to kiss him. And that wasn't the only time Clough became intimate with another man for the TV cameras. Once, in a live interview with ITV's Gary Newbon, Clough was asked why his team had played so badly. He replied: 'Because they're a bunch of pansies like you and me, Gary,' and kissed the startled presenter on the cheek before trotting off.

Forest finished eighth in 1991 and 1992, but Clough's health was in obvious decline and the following season they were relegated after finishing bottom of the table. It was the only time in Clough's twenty-eight years in management that he had experienced relegation, but the team was a poor one and by now he was in no state to work his motivational magic. His face was bloated and blotched. He looked jittery and often mumbled incoherently. The team had lost Webb to Manchester United, Walker to Sampdoria and Sheringham, their best striker, to Tottenham. Webb was brought back, but he remained either injured or not properly fit. The sale of Sheringham was incomprehensible to many – the season Forest went down he scored twenty-eight goals for Spurs. Clough claims that former Millwall striker Sheringham wanted to go back to London and that someone at Tottenham had 'tapped' him up. Whatever the reasons for Sheringham's departure, his replacement Robert Rosario was not in the same class and Forest managed just forty-one goals in forty-two games. Clough's captain Stuart Pearce, who was out for much of the season with injury, was by now blanking his manager completely after his refusal to discuss a new contract. Clough's empire on the banks of the Trent was crumbling around him and the barbarians of the First Division were hammering at the gates.

His loyal backroom staff tried frantically to shore up the problems but without Clough there was no clear leadership and Forest were a mess. 'The game was developing tactically, but Clough didn't believe in all that,' explains Alan Hill. 'He believed in motivation, but sometimes you just had to know whether the opposition played 4-4-2 or three at the back. Secretly we would try and find out all this and the first team coach would pass it on to Skipper [Stuart Pearce]. But the players had so much respect for him he never found out what was going on.'

Ronnie Fenton believes Clough was close to quitting at the end of the 1991 season. Clough had never won the FA Cup and his last chance was blown when they lost in the final to Tottenham that year after a late own goal by Des Walker. 'I think if we had won that then he would have retired then,' says Fenton. 'His health was not good. Brian obviously drank too much and that affected his health, no doubt about it.'

Clough's physical deterioration told its own story of his inner anguish. He looked awful. 'He really didn't know what he was doing at that stage,' admits John O'Hare. 'He was on another planet. I had not seen him in years and I couldn't believe how far downhill he had gone.' Some parts of the media began taking cheap shots at Clough; the satirical puppet programme *Spitting Image* lampooned him wobbling around his sitting room trying to arrange the bottles in his drinks cabinet into a team formation. At one time, no one would have dared ridicule the man so brazenly, but by the end of his career it was open day on Ol' Bighead.

The final knife was plunged by Forest director Chris Wooton, who went public with Clough's problems, telling a Sunday tabloid that the Forest manager was a drunk and that there had been a coup at the club to sack him. 'I don't know why he was talking about my drinking, because he was never at the ground,' says Clough today. 'The only thing he did for me was give me a shotgun – quite a good one, actually. I was only shooting rabbits at the time, but I should have used it to shoot him.'

Forest announced Clough's parting from the club five days before they were relegated by Sheffield United's victory at the City Ground. Clough's glittering career had come to a painfully inglorious end. Interviewed after the match, Clough, his face devastated by ill health and emotion, could barely speak. The bigmouth never short of a fresh and original comment for any occasion had lost his greatest gift – the power to enlighten and lift the spirits. A broken man, he stumbled down the corridor into the bowels of the stadium and, reeling with a mixture of emotions, picked up his young grandson in a replica Forest shirt and squeezed him tight to his chest.

Clough's retirement did not end the controversy that had dogged him throughout his career. His reputation was damaged when he was dragged into the 'bung' scandal sweeping English football after George

Graham's sacking from Arsenal for allegedly taking illegal payments for transfers. Allegations were made about Clough's business activities and the FA charged him with misconduct after a lengthy investigation. Clough denied all accusations before the FA let the matter drop over concern for his health.

Nottingham's most famous figure after Robin Hood has always been a strong family man, and in the comfort of their company he has slowly rebuilt his life, his health improving in recent years. His rapid and very public decline was a sad conclusion to a career that brought so much colour to English football over nearly three decades. History, though, will relegate those images to the foot of the page and it will be the younger, finger-wagging eccentric with the cocksure manner and hatful of homespun philosophy that will linger in the memory. For Brian Clough, football was a simple game: pass the ball and move into a new position; caress the ball, don't just punt it. His teams were always pleasing on the eye and always played the game fairly. Forest players were rarely sent off and they never dived.

John McGovern, his long-serving captain, could be speaking for a whole generation of football fans when he says: 'I was just grateful to be born in the same era as someone as brilliant as Clough. It was a hell of a ride, but I will always be extremely grateful.'

VINNIE JONES
NONE HARDER

When Vincent Peter Jones hung up his football boots and decided to embark on a career in acting, it came as little surprise to football fans to learn that he had been cast in the role of a gangster in his first film. One day, the theatre world might travel to Stratford-upon-Avon to watch Vinnie play Hamlet, or to the West End to see him perform Algernon in Oscar Wilde's *The Importance of Being Earnest*, but at the start of his new career he is taking the roles that come naturally to him. He plays hard men. Very convincingly. Does he make himself understood?

There were a few chuckles in pubs and football changing rooms up and down the country when the most feared and vilified British player of his generation decided that sitting in make-up and swapping anecdotes with his new thespian colleagues was the logical step forward. There was a time when a glamorous night out for

Vinnie Jones meant going to a curry house in Watford after a few pints down at his local with Dennis Wise and Dave Bassett. Today, you're just as likely to find him being photographed kissing Madonna at the premiere of a Hollywood blockbuster. After a career in football more notable for achievement in the disciplinary field than for aesthetic contribution, it has been frustrating for the sceptics to see the former Wimbledon scrapper picking up accolades for his performances on the silver screen. At the first screening of *Lock, Stock and Two Smoking Barrels*, the critics fixed their bayonets, sat back and waited for the expected assault on their artistic sensibilities. But as the credits rolled and the lights came up at the end, most of them were forced to concede that Jones had barely put a foot wrong in his big-screen debut.

There was a ring of authenticity to his performance as scary tough guy Big Chris; some even said that he was the star of the show. The most memorable moment of Jones's performance came when Big Chris killed another character by slamming his head in a car door. The key, apparently, was that Jones didn't actually act. He just played himself. When he went for his casting session, Jones understandably thought that the challenge of acting was trying to be someone that he wasn't. And it wasn't going very well until the casting director told him to relax and just be himself. Bingo. A star was born. You have to wonder if the casting director would have given Jones the same advice if he had been auditioning for Eric Cantona's part as the French ambassador in the highly acclaimed film *Elizabeth*. Seeing the former Manchester United idol smoothing around the screen in feathered cap, body-hugging tights and a fitted tunic was weird enough. But imagine Vinnie Jones in the same part and it's enough to make you reach for the smelling salts.

Vinnie's rapid rise to the higher echelons of celebrity society has been a source of surprise to many. Had he been playing a decade or so earlier he would have been no more than a common-or-garden football hard man who probably would have opened up a provincial pub after retiring. There was a time when you couldn't walk into a pub in Britain without having your pint pulled by a former Stoke City fullback or a Sheffield United midfield journeyman. Nowadays, such is the rising stock of the professional footballer that the likes of Vinnie Jones find themselves clinking champagne flutes with minor Royals and *EastEnders* stars at West End charity bashes. You can only imagine what Liverpool's Tommy Smith and Leeds's Norman Hunter, the hardest of an earlier generation of hard men, made of it all when they saw newspaper pictures of Vinnie poncing about with Sting at the launch of a Tibetan peace garden. And what on earth was he doing addressing undergraduates at the Oxford Union?

• • •

Whatever way you look at it – and whether you admire Vinnie Jones or not – his life has certainly been a remarkable one. And in a strange way, it's also an inspiration. He left school without any significant qualifications, drifted in and out of various poorly paid jobs and lived out of a plastic bag. Then, a chance encounter launched his career in football at a comparatively late age. Within a couple of years, Jones had become a household name, a byword for uncompromising aggression and commitment on the football pitch. Hundreds of more gifted players have not attracted a fraction of the attention enjoyed by Jones, who rose rapidly from non-league obscurity to the top flight of English football and even became the captain of an international team. When Jones finally walked away from the game, a new form of celebrity was almost instantly thrust upon him when he dared to try and become a film actor. Although racked by self-doubt throughout his adult life, Jones has become walking proof that courage and sheer bloody-mindedness can take a man of modest abilities an extremely long way. Jones goes to the place where most of us fear – or cannot be bothered – to tread: to the very limits of our abilities, the frontline of life's challenges.

It was easy to sneer at Jones the footballer with his US Marine crew cut, his permanent snarl, his clenched fists and the veins bursting out of his neck. He rarely lifted our spirits with a mazy dribble, a neat back-heel or delicate lob. And how often we winced when he scythed down a player or threw himself into a ruck. 'Typical,' everyone said, when he was sent off. But every football team needs a bastard – Leeds manager Don Revie used to say he wanted to create a whole team of them. Jones was by no stretch of the imagination one of the best players of his generation. Without any question, though, he was his generation's biggest and best footballing bastard, and he played a central role at Wimbledon in one of the most remarkable team success stories of the modern era.

Jones's ten-year spell at the top of the game was not without controversy. In a career that took him from Wealdstone to Holmsund in Sweden, then to Wimbledon, Leeds, Sheffield United, Chelsea, Wimbledon again and finally QPR, the boy from Watford was fined a total of £30,000, sent off thirteen times and twice booked within five seconds after the opening whistle. He also received a suspended six-month ban for fronting a video called *Soccer's Hard Men* – an historical celebration of the unsavoury, the unseemly and the downright horrible in football. In it, Vinnie generously hands out a series of tips to the nation's promising young thugs, including how to pull up a felled opponent by the armpit hair, scrape studs down the leg, elbow, poke eyes and crush testicles – without catching the ref's eye.

Other edited highlights of his misdemeanours include biting the nose of a reporter in Dublin a few hours after England's match with the Republic of Ireland at Lansdowne Road was abandoned. Towards the end of his playing days he was also handed 100 hours of community service after being found guilty of assaulting a neighbour whom he was accused of punching, kicking and biting.

But there is another side to Jones's personality that commentators rarely dwelled on for fear that it might soften the image of their cardboard cut-out caricature of a thug. Can he really be such a terrible person if he does so much work for good causes like SPARKS, the children's charity, and for Harefield Hospital? Can he really be a true bad boy after ten years of doting on his beloved wife, who needs constant monitoring since a heart transplant following complications giving birth? Is 'the folk hero of the battering classes', as he was described by one newspaper commentator, actually a bit soft?

Perhaps it's these contradictions that give Vinnie Jones his appeal: the capacity for extreme violence and extreme kindness, with nothing boring in between. He will threaten someone with the same passion that he puts into his charity work or family life. People like to get what they see, and if there's one thing that Vinnie Jones can't be accused of, it's pretending to be something he isn't. Even when he's acting.

By the age of thirty-six, he had already produced two hugely successful chronicles of his life. In his first autobiography, Jones summed up the way he saw himself as a footballer, and you can read the same sentiments into the way he has conducted himself in his wider life: 'I adopted that attitude that said: "I am from Watford, I'm off the building site and I'm representing the ordinary working-class folk of this country. I know all about the Eric Cantonas of this world, with all their dosh. Great player but we're not all born like that. We've not all been so lucky. Some of us have had to work bloody hard to make it this far."'

The only ironic thing about this statement of faith in himself is that Jones should contrast himself with Eric Cantona. Certainly, there was a big gulf in their skills and their earnings, but in other ways they have much in common. Both were dedicated professionals, both were proud to the point of explosion, both were prone to the red mist, both were dogged by controversy throughout their careers and both surprised everyone by swapping a career in football for one in cinema.

• • •

Jones caught the eye of football scouts as a youngster first with his local club Bedmond in Hertfordshire and then as captain of Watford schools. Aged fourteen, he joined Watford, at a time when future England manager Graham Taylor and club owner Elton John were in the process of transforming the unfashionable club into a significant football power, taking them from the depths of the Fourth Division to the First. As one of the best young players from the local area, Jones had high hopes of making the grade at Vicarage Road, but he was soon released and told he wasn't good enough to compete at the highest level. The news, broken to him by Bertie Mee, the former Arsenal manager who was in charge of youth teams at Watford, couldn't have come at a more difficult time for Jones. His parents' marriage was disintegrating – a traumatic experience for a child at any age, but it hit Jones particularly hard as he headed into the confusing, character-forging years of early adolescence. Jones had loved his childhood until the period leading up to his parents' break-up, when he would sit at top of stairs with his arm around his little sister Ann as they listened to their mother and father arguing. His rejection by Watford and the end of his childhood innocence came as a double body blow to the emotional teenager whose eyes were only just being opened to the harsher realities of adult life.

Jones developed a special relationship with his father, whom he lived with after his mother re-married, but like many aimless teenagers he soon drifted into a life of truancy and trouble. They ended up falling out and didn't speak to each other for three years. After leaving school at the first available opportunity, Jones floated from one poorly paid, menial job to another, living out of a bin liner and earning enough money to keep him in food and beer. He worked as a general labourer and washed pots and pans at Bradfield public school. He also shaved off his hair and got his ear pierced – nothing unusual about that, you might think, except for the fact that he pierced it himself. During this time, Jones started to develop a reputation as bit of a Jack the Lad, not shy of a high-street dust-up at chucking-out time. When he wasn't working, the young Vinnie spent his free time pubbing, clubbing and scrapping, often enjoying all three activities in one evening. But despite a number of brushes with the local constabulary, he never landed himself in serious trouble. Losing his licence for drink driving was the only official entry on his police record.

Jones took a job as a groundsman at Bushey College, mowing lawns and white-lining the pitches. Semi-professional Conference team Wealdstone came to train at the ground one day and, short of players, the coach invited Jones to make up the numbers. Wealdstone were one of most highly regarded non-league teams in the country and could even boast future England fullback Stuart Pearce amongst their old boys. It was an opportunity that the talented, aggressive young foot-baller, disillusioned with his life as a drifter, was not going to pass up. He made a big impression that day and was soon taken on to Wealdstone's books for a nominal weekly wage. His physical strength and combative qualities were highly prized in the blood baths of non-league football and he quickly gained a reputation as a player not to be fooled with. Nor did he waste much time in familiarizing himself with the league's referees. A Vinnie Jones challenge in an FA Cup match against Reading sparked a massive free-for-all, and he was sent off against Weymouth after another fight. His former team-mates affectionately remember 'Jonesy', or 'Jonah', as a 'complete nutcase'.

Through Wimbledon manager Dave Bassett, whom he knew from his youth in Bedmond and who would become a major influence on his life and career, Jones secured a contract to play with Swedish side Holmsund in 1986. The club were nothing in international terms – in fact, they were very little in Swedish terms, being in the third division, northern section – but Jones became a minor folk hero in Sweden. When he arrived for training at the remote club in the frozen north of the country he must have looked like Steptoe Junior, clutching all his worldly possessions in a bin liner. Jones would enjoy a standard of living in Sweden he had never previously experienced, and it gave him a taste for a better life. He was paid good money, given a free car and accommodation, and treated with respect and affection by both his team-mates and the local people.

Holmsund would be the making of Jones as a footballer. It was there that his confidence returned and he realized he had something to offer the game – and it had something to offer him in return. Jones had acquitted himself well at Wealdstone, establishing a reputation as a ferociously competitive midfielder with a gift for inspiring his team-mates. At Holmsund he showed all of those qualities, and he was also one of the team's most skilful players, so he stood out. It wasn't only that Jones began to believe in himself as a player, but more importantly, he began to believe in himself as a person, and he realized that he could put his strong personality to work as a means to further his career. The other players looked up to him and respected his courage, feeding off his demonic commitment to the cause. His fame reached its height when he inspired a run that saw the part-timers reach the semi-finals of the Swedish equivalent of the FA Cup.

Jones was having the time of his life in the frozen wilderness of northern Scandinavia and word had got back to England – or at least to Dave Bassett at Wimbledon – that the Watford reject had created a minor stir. He was preparing to settle in Holmsund for the short-term future but at the end of his first season he was invited for a trial at the Dons, who had just completed their remarkable twelve-year surge from non-league obscurity to the top flight of arguably the hardest league in world football. Once again Jones seized the opportunity of a leg-up to a higher level and after four weeks on the training ground he was handed a contract.

Rarely do footballers spring from total anonymity into the public limelight. Normally they have to work their way through a club's youth and reserve teams, or battle their way to prominence in the lower divisions of the Football League. Coincidentally, Stuart Pearce was another Wealdstone graduate to buck the system. Both would end up as international captains and prove to hundreds of non-league foot-ballers that anything is possible. For Jones, the key to his success was Bassett, a man he likes to describe as 'a god in my life'.

Jones didn't take long to jump to national attention. Millions of *Match of the Day* viewers saw him score on his home debut against Manchester United with a towering header that won the match for the south London side. Wimbledon was a club built in Jones's image. Their extraordinary progress was built not on outrageous talent but on brute determination, the simplicity and honesty of the players' tactical approach and their intimidation of technically superior opponents. They were dubbed 'The Crazy Gang', and their belligerence on the pitch and antics off it made them a celebrated, if not always well-loved, institution. Jones, John 'Fash the Bash' Fashanu, Dennis 'The Menace' Wise and Eric 'Ninja' Young were the most colourful characters on a team sheet that read like a *Viz* version of the Roy of the Rovers cartoon strip. They were the boys from nowhere, earning a fraction of the fees that their rivals could command, and with facilities no better than a local school. Yet they became a match for the biggest teams in the land. You could say what you liked about the quality of their football – Wimbledon didn't care. They knew they were an extraordinary achievement, an inspiration to every small club dreaming of glory.

Jones quickly established himself as an essential part of Wimbledon's mean machine and, inevitably as the hard man of the hardest team in the top flight, it wasn't long before he was given his first early bath. Graham Rix, Arsenal's skilful former England midfielder, criticized the Dons in the press, stating that their crude style of football had no place in one of Europe's elite leagues. Jones sought him out from the first whistle, left him lying in a heap on the ground at the first opportunity and was promptly dispatched.

After a brief spell in the Conference with Wealdstone and a year in the Swedish third division, Jones was largely innocent in the ways of the media, particularly the tabloid newspapers. He had always spoken frankly and honestly, but his candour and naiveté soon landed him his first full-blown scandal after he gave an interview in the *Sun* revealing that he had told Liverpool idol Kenny Dalglish that he was going to 'rip off his ear and spit down the hole' during an on-pitch altercation. The story was plastered over the back page of Britain's best-selling newspaper and immediately picked up by other media

networks. On the morning the story hit the news-stands a mob of journalists and camera crews descended on Wimbledon's training ground
off the A3 in south-west London.

Later in the 1987/88 season, Jones's image as a thug was fixed in
the minds of English footballers forever following the publication of one
photograph in virtually every newspaper in the country. The picture,
taken during a league match against Newcastle, made Jones a household name and has become one of the most infamous images in football. Jones had been detailed to shadow Paul Gascoigne, then a young
midfielder of outstanding promise, who had destroyed Wimbledon at
their last meeting with the range of his passing and skills. Jones took
his brief very seriously, telling Gascoigne that he was going to mark him
so tightly he would follow him into the toilet if he had to. True to his
word, Jones shadowed Gazza around the pitch like a pit-bull, squeez-
ing out every bit of space in which the future England star might wreak
havoc. Gascoigne's frustration was mounting by the minute. Then, to
cap it all, he received the surprise of his footballing life as Jones backed
into him at a set-piece. Gazza was looking out for the ball when the
Wimbledon hard man, his face contorted in vicious concentration,
reached behind him, took his opponent's wedding tackle in a vice-like
grip and gave it a good tug.

The picture of the incident shows Gazza bending forward in agony.
He reportedly left the field in tears, and the following day the papers
were full of righteous indignation over Jones's behaviour. From that
one moment, captured for eternity by a hawk-eyed photographer,
Vinnie Jones's image as a hoodlum was set in stone. And from then
on, every football journalist would be on the lookout for another story.

The press didn't have to wait long for their next Vinnie horror story.
In his very next game, against Everton at Goodison Park, Jones

clashed with England's Peter Reid, a hard man himself and a player with whom he would have a string of eye-watering confrontations throughout his career (Jones also had a long-running power struggle with Liverpool's Steve McMahon, another pitiless, uncompromising midfield enforcer). The pair collided heavily, and with the Everton man sprawled on the floor, Jones dived in for more, shoving his boot into Reid's face. The hot bath beckoned and off he went, with a blast of moral outrage at his back.

The full extent of Wimbledon's extraordinary rise in status was brought home when they reached the final of the FA Cup, the oldest and most venerable domestic cup competition in international football. Hundreds of millions of viewers from around the world would now have the chance to see the Crazy Gang phenomenon for themselves as the Dons lined up against the aristocrats of English football – Liverpool. The four-times European champions were still the most revered club side in the world, despite the ban on English clubs in Europe following the Heysel Stadium disaster. The Merseysiders boasted a fabulous array of talent including John Barnes, Peter Beardsley, John Aldridge and Alan Hansen, and they were widely expected to brush aside their competition, who had grown too big for their unsponsored boots.

Wimbledon, now under Bobby Gould, had other ideas. Their plan was no different to any other match: they were going to intimidate, harass and spoil their celebrated opponents into humiliating submission. Jones's brief was simple: get the better of his opposite man McMahon, so that the Dons could control the midfield and kill off Liverpool's supply routes to their dangerous front runners.

The press were caught in two minds in the build-up to the Wembley showdown. On the one hand it was considered wonderful for the game that a club that had been non-league just over a decade ago could be just ninety minutes away from lifting the trophy by beating a team of international superstars. At one level, this was the stuff of Roy of the Rovers, barely credible in the real world. Others, however, failed to see any romance in the scenario and questioned whether it would reflect well on the quality of English football – or if it was good for football's soul – if a team so limited in skill and so crude in its tactics could win the title.

Not that Wimbledon and Jones cared about the debate. Their minds were set rigid on winning the match by whatever means it took, even if that meant boring the pants off a global television audience. The Liverpool players – and those watching from home – were given an early glimpse of Wimbledon's determination not to pass up what, more likely than not, would be the opportunity of a lifetime. As the teams prepared to emerge from the tunnel to a wall of noise from the 99,000-strong crowd, the Wimbledon players started screaming like banshees and eyeballing their opponents. Liverpool were not a team to suffer from pre-match nerves, and there was barely a challenge that they had not risen to and met head on over the last decade. To this day, Hansen and his team deny they were in the least bit moved by Wimbledon's tribal war-cry – but you can't help but think that they must have been at least slightly rattled.

Midway through the first half, Jones got his first chance to crunch McMahon. McMahon was one of the hardest players of his generation and vilified by opposition fans up and down the country. (Chelsea supporters particularly enjoyed taunting this symbol of muscular machismo by chanting 'Steve McMahon is a homosexual' in monotonous repetition throughout a match in a bid to try and wind him up and get him sent off.) Jones came crashing in on him, the Liverpool player flew into the air and, as he landed, his elbow caught Jones in the eye, opening a wound just underneath it. It was a titanic clash of the two most feared players on the pitch. As a statement of Wimbledon's demonic determination and their lack of respect for their more illustrious opponents, Jones's challenge could not have been bettered. If that tackle alone didn't win the midfield, it did at least shake up the Liverpool ranks, who began to get rid of the ball with greater urgency, upsetting their composure and the rhythm of their passing.

Shortly afterwards, Wimbledon scored when Lawrie Sanchez rose to glance a free kick beyond the stranded Liverpool goalkeeper Bruce Grobbelaar. There was bedlam amongst the Wimbledon players and fans, as well as amongst neutrals up and down the country, hoping that England's dominant club side of the past ten years would receive an embarrassing slapdown. The only people wearing a look of dejection were the Liverpool players – and goal scorer Sanchez. In what has since been described as the worst goal celebration in history, Sanchez barely raised a smile, frozen to the turf as if he had put it into his own net and wrecked his side's chances of victory.

There followed one of the most famous moments in FA Cup history. Liverpool were awarded a penalty. No one had ever missed a spot kick in the final and John Aldridge, who calmly stepped up to place the ball, was one of the best exponents of the nerve-racking art in the game. It seemed as if the momentum of the match had finally and decisively swung behind the favourites. But Aldridge missed – Wimbledon goalkeeper Dave Beasant flung his huge frame to the left and palmed the ball around the post. Liverpool had blown a perfect chance to level the match and wrest back the initiative. It was to be Wimbledon's day after all, and at the final whistle Jones went beserk, haring around the pitch, punching the air and screaming at his friends and fans in the crowd. After collecting his medal from Princess Diana, Jones continued to run around the Wembley turf like a maniac, veins bursting out of his head, thrusting his medal at the crowd. Bobby Gould came onto the pitch to urge restraint, calling on his players to show some dignity in victory. Perhaps Jones didn't quite catch what Gould had asked him to show – at the team photograph the almost hysterical hard man cupped his manhood through his shorts and shoved it towards the face of his startled manager.

This was to be the highlight of Jones's playing career, and he was going to milk every moment of it. And why not? How many of us can boast an FA Cup winner's medal? Following the obligatory bus tour in south London the following day, Jones launched himself into a week of celebrations. Three years earlier, he had cut a lonely and down-at-heel figure as he mowed the pitches at Bushey College. Now he was one of the best-known faces in British sport – and a winner to boot.

• • •

If the 1987/88 season ended in glory, the subsequent campaign began in shame when Jones was sent off in a pre-season friendly on the Isle of Wight following a mass brawl. Gould was not impressed and banned him indefinitely, raising doubts about the manager's respect for his volatile midfield scrapper. Jones missed the Charity Shield, in which Liverpool avenged their FA Cup defeat with a 2-1 win, but when he was restored to the squad, it wasn't long before he found himself back in what was slowly becoming his second home – the doghouse. In a match against Tottenham, Jones launched himself into England international Gary Stevens, who crumpled in agony under the force of the challenge. Although it would be months before the full extent of the damage was clear, Stevens' knee was wrecked and his career was over. To this day Jones maintains there was no malice in the tackle. Once again, he found himself cast as the thug of English football, whose brutality had brought an end to the career of a fellow footballer.

Gould's patience was wearing thin, but it snapped altogether later in the season during a match with Everton. Jones went in late on Scotland striker Graham Sharp and as Everton players rushed to the scene, Kevin Ratcliffe, a hard man in his own right, confronted Jones. The pair squared up, toe to toe, and then bang! Ratcliffe was lying on the ground, clutching his face. Jones claimed that he never head-butted the Welshman – but with a record like his, who was ever going to believe him? Jones had made it easy for people to be judgmental about his conduct, and there was never likely to be much sympathy for his cries of innocence.

Vinnie Jones was a much-loved figure at Wimbledon – in many ways he seemed to represent all it stood for – but his incorrigible indis-cipline brought a stream of negative headlines, and the club took the painful decision to offload him. Gould, who never had the same admi-ration for Jones's abilities as his predecessor Bassett, sold him to Leeds, where his combative, galvanizing skills would be highly prized. Leeds, then languishing in the Second Division, knew that the best way into the top flight was to battle rather than entertain their way there, and they jumped at the chance of signing him. They needed a scrapper and scrappers came no better than Vinnie 'Bite Yer Legs' Jones. They like a hard man in Leeds – Billy Bremner, Norman Hunter, Jack Charlton, Johnny Giles and David Batty remain revered figures at the club.

Leeds gave Jones generous personal terms, trebling his wages and providing him with a state-of-the-art BMW. The Yorkshire club may have been in a lower division than Wimbledon, but they were in differ-ent league when it came to resources and tradition. Jones took one step down in a football sense but jumped several flights of stairs in terms of his personal circumstances. Not everyone at the club thought his arrival was great news, though. 'I just thought he was a big thug with a long throw,' says Gordon Strachan, who joined the club around the same time. It took time for Jones to settle in to his new environment and build up friendships with his new team-mates. He missed the camaraderie and the happy atmosphere of the Wimbledon changing room as well as the company of his friends and family down south. Leeds had brought in a number of new players as they prepared to launch a major promotion campaign, including Strachan, Mel Sterland and Mickey Thomas, while youngsters like Gary Speed and Batty were starting to press their claims from the junior ranks. A rift soon opened up between the new faces and the more established players and Jones, used to the 'one-for-all, all-for-one' atmosphere of Wimbledon, couldn't stand the tension and the lack of solidarity.

After one training session he snapped when Bobby Davison, one of the senior Leeds players, said to him: 'You do know we pass to feet here.' It was a slight not just on Jones's ability as a footballer but also on his beloved Wimbledon, the academy of so-called 'Route One' football he had just left and missed so much. Jones's response had an eloquence and clarity of meaning that words simply couldn't have expressed. He flattened Davison with a punch in the mouth before enquiring of the rest of the players whether any of them 'would like some'. There were no takers, and with that one blow Vinnie had established a new order of authority in the changing room. The new boys weren't going to take any shit. Far from being reprimanded, the Leeds management quietly welcomed Jones's action. This was why they had brought him in. He was a leader who would silence the moaners as well as unite and inspire the dressing room by his will to win and his aggression. Strachan, the captain, was the most influential player on the pitch that season, but Jones's contribution to morale was equally significant.

That 1989/90 season was probably the best of Jones's entire career, purely in football terms, and he quickly established himself as a crowd favourite. He developed a particularly close rapport with the disabled fans, whom he always made of point of chatting to on match days. Cynics might say that Jones excelled because standards were lower in the Second Division and he was rarely left feeling frustrated or humiliated by technically superior players getting the better of him. But one must also factor in the influence of manager Howard Wilkinson and Jones's skipper Strachan, who went out of their way to boost his confidence, encouraging him to move his game up to a higher level, to pass and create as well as to chase and spoil.

His growing confidence was reflected in the fact that he was only booked twice and was not sent off over the entire season. The only trouble Jones landed himself in while he was at Leeds occurred away from the pitch, when he was arrested following a fight outside a nightclub. The story appeared in the *Sun* and Jones was carpeted by Wilkinson and other Leeds officials, who had recently launched a campaign to purge the club of its hooligan and racist elements.

Leeds secured promotion with victory at Bournemouth, sparking wild celebrations back in the streets and bars of the Yorkshire city. Jones had played a key role in the club's return to the elite, and by the end of the season he was feeling as good about himself as a footballer as he ever had done. He had been given every reason to expect he would continue to play a major part in the club's plans for the following season, not least because he already had two years of experience in the First Division. So when he heard, during the close season, that the club had bought Gary McAllister from Leicester, Jones was devastated. He knew exactly what the arrival of the skilful Scottish midfielder meant: he was on his way out – or at very best, on his way into the reserves. It seemed that Leeds, ruthless in their pursuit of glory, had brought in Jones for one mission only – to help the club fight their way out of the battlefields of the Second Division. Mission accomplished. If survival for the next season or two had been Leeds's sole aim, then they would almost certainly have retained the services of a man so used to scrapping for his living on a football pitch. But Leeds signalled their intentions of an immediate challenge to the bigger clubs by signing up recruits with more specialist skills. Jones's speciality was to get stuck into the opposition, but with Batty, Speed, Strachan and now McAllister in their midfield ranks, they had four players who were both tough and skilful.

If Jones felt insecure about the quality of his 'purer' football skills, those demons of self-doubt had been exorcized in that one season at Leeds. But the implication that he was not up to competing at the highest level with a team that had just won promotion shattered the confidence he had built up over the previous twelve months. Jones didn't go immediately, but when Sheffield United, then bottom of the Second Division, came in for him, there seemed little point in refusing a lucrative offer of first-team football. His old friend and mentor Dave Bassett was their manager and, like Wilkinson at Leeds, he knew that his protegé was the man to help the club fight their way out of trouble. But the Leeds fans' affection for Jones endured and on his return to Elland Road later in his career, he was given a standing ovation. In his autobiography, he says that a steward told him only one other former player had been accorded a similar tribute: the great John Charles.

Jones didn't enjoy himself at Sheffield United, a poor team compared to Leeds, but he did what he was brought in to do. The club avoided the drop. Jones was never sent off at Sheffield, but his discipline deteriorated a little, mainly because he was playing in a team that more often than not was chasing opposition sides rather than dominating them. A team without possession of the ball risks committing fouls in its efforts to retrieve it; it's difficult to foul an opponent when you're busy passing, scoring or moving into a space. The most notable booking of his career to date came against Manchester City, when he was booked after just five seconds for a challenge on – guess who? – Peter Reid.

During his time at Sheffield United, Jones's girlfriend Mylene gave birth to their son Aaron, a happy event in an otherwise mildly depressing spell at the south Yorkshire club. When they returned down south, Jones was keen to follow. He had wanted to be closer to his friends and family anyway, but now that he had a young son there too, the pull was even greater. When Chelsea called United and put in an offer for him, Jones was only too keen to accept, even if it meant that he would be playing for his fourth club in as many years. Bassett, his father-figure, thanked him for fulfilling the job he had been asked to do – namely to put a bit of bite in the midfield and a bit of spirit in the dressing room – and sent him on his way.

Jones's spell at Chelsea, who were then in the Second Division, was memorable mainly for events off the field. Soon after joining the west London club, he got into a fight at a taxi rank with someone who proved he could match the famous hard man of football blow for blow. Jones ended up with stitches in his head as well as a thick ear, but by all accounts gave at least as good as he got. Vinnie was back in town, just in case we hadn't heard.

He also set an English football record that will surely never be broken when he managed to get booked after just *three* seconds in an FA Cup match against his former club Sheffield United at Stamford Bridge, shaving a whole two seconds off his personal best. Barely had the referee finished blowing his whistle to get the game underway when Jones bundled into Dean Whitehouse, leaving him in a crumpled heap on the turf. But Jones found himself in even more serious trouble when he was hauled before an FA disciplinary panel and fined £1,500 for making a hand gesture to Arsenal fans at Highbury. Jones claimed he was having a laugh with a friend in the crowd, but the panel declined to believe him, openly wondering why anyone might want to greet an old friend that way.

But the most significant episode in this period was Jones's reunion with a childhood friend, Tanya Lamont, with whom he fell madly in love. At first, Tanya, who had been in a relationship with Watford's Steve Terry, struggled to see the attractive side of her new suitor. But she was soon won over as Jones revealed aspects of his character wholly different from his public image as a football warrior or a night-club fight waiting to happen. Tanya had undergone heart transplant surgery following the birth of her daughter Kaley, and her condition needed close monitoring. During one of her frequent visits to hospital, Jones was a tower of strength and comfort, sitting by her bedside for hours holding her hand – not to mention looking after Kaley and running the household in her absence. The hard nut had a soft centre; Tanya was smitten. In 1994 they married at a lavish ceremony in their new Hertfordshire home, which Jones had had built for them to move into after their honeymoon.

By then, Jones had packed his kit bag once again and returned to Wimbledon, where he was greeted like a long-lost hero – and it seemed just like old times when he was given his marching orders on his home debut after clattering the Irishman Kevin Moran and giving him an earful of industrial abuse. It must have been something in the air or water in south London – Jones hadn't been sent off since he left Wimbledon over five years earlier.

Far greater trouble was brewing, however. A newly released video, entitled *Soccer's Hard Men*, featured Jones giving advice on how to successfully damage an opponent without being spotted by the referee. More torture training manual than wholesome football tips, the video caused a storm of outrage, and the BBC felt shaken enough by the horror of it all to have it included amongst the lead items in its *Nine O'Clock News* bulletin. To this day, Jones claims he is filled with remorse for being so naive as to get involved in the project, for which he received only a small fee. He pleaded his case with the FA, but the tired, familiar faces sitting on the disciplinary panel were not swayed by the protestations of innocence from the Wimbledon One. Football's governing body could not be seen to show lenience over the issue of violence and foul play, and they wanted to send out a message – particularly to young footballers – that they would not tolerate the promotion of such vicious behaviour. Jones received a record £20,000 fine and a six-month ban, suspended for three years. There were many who felt he had escaped lightly. For his critics, bad tackles in the heat of a football battle were one thing, but the celebration of brutality in the cold light of a day off was quite another.

Jones's life was already in danger of turning into a circus when he made his first foray into show business with an appearance on *Gladiators*. For a first role in a non-football television programme, *Gladiators* was perfect: nothing too serious, no lines to remember; just make scary faces and beat the guy up. Vinnie clearly fancied it as he strode onto the set to show them what it meant to be really tough. But it all 'kicked off' and Vinnie, for once, found himself on the receiving end of a mauling. The other contestants had decided to target him and he was set upon by men in colourful shorts and padded headgear. Vinnie, whose temper was hanging by a gossamer thread by the end of his struggle, had scored precisely zero points and he marched off set looking as if he was going to turn the hospitality room upside down. But his injured pride got the better of him and as the Saturday prime-time audience looked on in amazement, he returned to the set and started a full-scale brawl, single-handedly turning a harmless family TV show into something altogether more menacing. For a brief moment, mayhem reigned and you wondered whether the police might have to be called, before the curtain was quickly and mercifully brought down on Vinnie's showbiz debut.

The mid-1990s was a troubled period for Jones – both on and off the pitch. In the 1994/95 season he was sent off against Leicester for fighting, and again against Newcastle for a nauseating tackle on Rob Lee. But, despite the apparent deterioration in his discipline, at the same time Jones became an international footballer when it was discovered that he qualified for Wales through his paternal grandfather. Jones was delighted and headed straight to the nearest tattoo artist, who added the Welsh motif of dragon and feathers to the tattoos celebrating Wimbledon's FA Cup win and Leeds's promotion to the First Division. Jones wasted little time in showing the world that no player in the international football community was now safe from a good clobbering. He was sent off against Georgia in 1995 after he mowed down an opponent and – just for good measure – stood on him. That moment of mania cost him a five-month ban and even the neo-Welshman, on seeing the television evidence, was forced to concede that there had probably been an infringement of the rules.

The dismissal came just a few months after an incident in a Dublin hotel lounge that caused widespread outrage, the fall-out from which would send Jones into a deep depression. England's 'friendly' against the Republic of Ireland at Lansdowne Road was abandoned after a group of right-wing hooligans began ripping up seats and hurling them onto the crowd below, all the while singing 'No Surrender to the IRA'. It was one of the worst outbreaks of violence involving England fans in years and the game was immediately plunged into gloom and recriminations again. Jones did little to enhance the reputation of the British abroad when, a few hours after the match was abandoned, he assaulted a *Mirror* reporter at a hotel where he had been drinking. Ted Oliver was introduced to Jones and, after a bit of horseplay, Jones grabbed him by the head and sunk his teeth into his nose, drawing blood. Jones allegedly apologized to Oliver later and had largely forgotten about the episode by the time he arrived back at Stansted airport nursing a hangover the following morning – to be confronted by a scrum of press and photographers. The story appeared on the front page of the *Mirror* and one of the headlines read: 'Vinnie fixed me with his teeth and shook me like a dog with a dead rabbit.' 'My biggest worry for days after was that I would get some kind of infection,' Oliver recalls. 'You can take the man out of the gutter, but you cannot take the gutter out of the man.' No matter what way you looked at it, Jones had bitten a man's nose. There could be no 'What me, ref?' claims of innocence. 'It was like watching a dog with a bone,' said former FA press officer Mike Parry.

Jones was genuinely shaken by his own behaviour – not to mention the media reaction that followed it – and was devastated at the thought that the stress of it all might undermine Tanya's health. He plunged into a depression so deep that he decided the only answer was to take his own life. After sending his wife out to do some shopping, Jones took his shotgun and walked out into the woods near his home. He sat down on an old oil barrel and drifted off into a kind of melancholic trance, fingering his gun. He was saved by the sound of his Jack Russell foraging in the bushes, which snapped him out of his stupor. He realized that his suicide would serve only to heap even more despair on Tanya and so he returned to his house and locked his gun away.

Jones came to terms with the misery that followed the Dublin incident and any worries that he may have lost his appetite for the fray were dispelled when he managed to get himself sent off three times before the end of the year, once playing for Wales against Georgia and twice for Wimbledon, against Nottingham Forest and Chelsea. His victim at Stamford Bridge was former World Player of the Year Ruud Gullit, whom he left writhing on the deck like a freshly landed cod. But the controversy didn't end with his red card. After the match, far from showing any remorse over the tackle, Jones told reporters he was fed up with 'foreign players squealing like pot-bellied pigs'. When asked by an *Observer* journalist at the end of his career how it was he still managed to get into such scrapes in his thirties, when it seemed that he was so sensible and mature – and charitable – in other areas of his life, Jones replied: 'I can only take so much sometimes. It does-n't matter who it is, every celebrity gets it. What they think is, you won't hit them because you've got your hands tied. But I'm the f**king opposite because I will f**king do it. I don't give a f**k.'

We have been warned. So was England forward Darren Anderton in the 1996/97 season, when he made the mistake of spitting within spitting distance of Vinnie. Jones chased him around the park for the rest of the match before he finally managed to get in a good wild lunge on him. Anderton denied he had deliberately cleared his catarrh in Jones's direction and the latter gave him the benefit of the doubt. 'If I saw him actually spitting at me, he would have been rearranged,' he says.

Jones's playing career came to an end at First Division QPR, yet another team who had turned to him when the good times had dried up and life had become no more than a grim battle for survival. He took on the role of player/assistant coach and was eyeing up the manager's position there when the possibility of an entirely different career presented itself in the form of a part in a major feature film. Tough decision, that: Rotherham on a wintry Tuesday night, or Sunset Boulevard in an open-top limo?

But first, there was the small matter of a criminal court case to be dealt with. Jones faced charges of actual bodily harm and criminal damage following a bust-up with his neighbour, Timothy Gear. St Albans Magistrates Court heard that Jones had bitten, kicked, punched and stamped on Gear in a row over a wooden stile. A forensic pathologist told the court that he could see no evidence of injuries caused by biting, stamping or kicking, but Jones was found guilty all the same and a jail sentence seemed likely. Unsurprisingly, therefore, Jones could hardly contain his delight when he was only landed with 100 hours' community service – painting an old people's home – and a £1,000 fine. He remained a free man and the rest is theatrical history.

• • •

Critics have found it easy to scoff at Jones the footballer, and he has often made himself a target. On the field, he may not have had the crowd rising to their feet in admiration at his breathtaking skills, but

Jones fulfilled a very important role, doing the dirty work that allowed the more ostentatiously talented players to flourish. Artisans need a strong man to carry the bricks. Jones was essentially a spoiler, an intimidator and a galvanizer whose energy, aggression and force of personality could disrupt the finest midfields in the business. He has gone on record several times to say how much this limited view of his talents galls him, how he hated being pigeonholed and caricatured by the media to whom he was one thing and one thing only: a player of incredible hardness who had nothing 'positive' or creative to offer the game, except an endless stream of easy newspaper copy. Jones's disciplinary record is indefensible but, like Roy Keane and Patrick Vieira, he was the type of player who would always be most at risk of being cautioned and dismissed. Yellow and red cards come with the territory.

Away from the pitch, Jones the man is a far more complex and beguiling character. Violence has been a part of his life there too, but with the exception of his victims, it is difficult to find a person with a harsh word to say about him. The tenderness with which he looks after his family and friends and the time he devotes to charity work is difficult to square with the more vicious side of his character. The only conclusion you can reach is that, like many men of passion and pride, Vinnie Jones is a character of multiple contradictions, capable of the greatest kindness as well as thuggery. A tough guy with a good heart, happy to punch someone's face in before popping out to do some charity work. A smashing bloke, in all senses of the word.

ALEX FERGUSON
THE GOVERNOR

When Sir Alex Ferguson finally walks away from football management, leaving behind a trail of broken teacups and glittering silverware, and an epidemic of tinnitus, he will do so happy in the knowledge that he will be remembered as the most successful manager in the 130-year history of organized British football. Or will he? 'I've never, ever seen him happy,' says Scottish football writer Hugh Keevins, 'because each day is a fresh challenge for him. Nostalgia doesn't play a great part in his life.'

Ferguson, a reasonably good player frustrated by lack of pace, has lifted over thirty trophies in a managerial career that spanned four decades, beginning in the backwaters of East Stirlingshire and ending at Manchester United, where he presided over the richest and best-supported club on the planet like a benevolent dictator. He didn't hold press conferences or team talks – he held court while journalists and players alike knelt at his feet. A man driven by an almost demonic urgency to get the better of others, Ferguson brooked no criticism of his autocratic approach to management. Even when he appeared to have overstepped the bounds of reasonable discipline by castigating David Beckham for missing training to look after his sick child, there was barely a whisper of criticism. No one, it seemed, not even an ailing toddler, was more important than Manchester United Football Club with Sir Alex in charge.

But it would be unfair to portray the Glaswegian as just a hard man with a fiery temper, oversimplifying a highly complex man whose public image has always been at odds with his private persona. Those close to Ferguson unanimously speak of him as a kind, generous, humble, loyal and funny man. In short, nothing like the granite-faced NCO character who appears on our television screens, always, it seems, on the point of volcanic eruption.

• • •

Alexander Chapman Ferguson was born in Govan, Glasgow, on New Year's Day 1941 and, like most young boys in the west of Scotland, all he wanted to do was play football for Glasgow Rangers or Celtic. Ferguson, who was descended from mixed religious stock but brought up a Protestant, gravitated towards Rangers and on Saturdays he would climb the walls of Ibrox to get a glimpse of his heroes. (Ferguson always despised the religious bigotry and bitter sectarianism that traditionally characterized the relationship between Glasgow's two great clubs.) He took a job at the shipyards on the Clyde as an apprentice tool worker until he was twenty-three years old, while playing part-time as centre-forward for Queens Park and St Johnstone. In 1964 he turned professional and joined Dunfermline before moving to Rangers in 1967 for £65,000, an enormous sum of money in the transfer market of the day.

He was a tough, hard-working striker and he acquitted himself well at the club he worshipped as a boy, but he was sold on to Falkirk two years later after an unhappy period during which he had to suffer the humiliation of being demoted to the third team. The reasons for his departure remain in dispute. Some say it was simply because he lacked the pace to become a truly outstanding striker, but others felt his removal involved something altogether more sinister: he had married a Catholic girl at a time when many people in the club, including the influential club official Willie Allison, still frowned upon such 'mixed marriages'. Ferguson was deeply upset by his alienation from the club he had followed so passionately for as long as he could remember and he spent the last four years of his playing career on the second rung of Scottish football at Falkirk and Ayr. While at Rangers he had become involved in the players' union, urging his colleagues to make a stand for their rights. The twin experiences of work in the shipyards and the camaraderie of the football changing room had taught Ferguson every-thing he needed to know about hard graft, solidarity and unity. 'He was a very passionate socialist back then,' says veteran *Glasgow Herald* reporter Ken Gallacher.

Ferguson has carried the indelible stamp of his upbringing like a tattoo all his working life and for all the money he now earns, he has never forgotten his roots. 'He is a product of his environment,' says Ian McGarry, a sports journalist who has followed Ferguson's career closely. 'Here's a man with more money than he could probably ever spend, mixing in horse-racing circles – a very upper-class sport – but there's no question of him turning his back on his background. He's never lost his accent and you get the feeling that a lot of what makes him tick is where he comes from. He has this image as a wee Glasgow hard man who has had to fight his way through.'

Within months of retiring as a player, in 1974 Ferguson embarked on a career in football management with East Stirlingshire, as provincial and insignificant a club as you could wish to find in the British Isles, a thousand light years removed from the galaxy of stars he would find himself amongst at Manchester United twelve years later. His talent was quickly spotted and within a year he was sitting in the manager's office at St Mirren. Ferguson threw himself into the challenge of reviving the moribund Paisley club with an enthusiasm and determination that delighted the club's followers and amazed neutral observers. 'He had this incredible energy,' recalls Glen Gibbons, Chief Football Writer at *The Scotsman* and friend of Ferguson. 'His daily schedule was horrifying: take the boys to school, check one of his pubs, go to Love Street to take training, check the pubs again, pick up the boys, home for an hour, back to Love Street for training with the youth teams, go to a game, and then back to the pubs to check everything was all right.'

In a bid to encourage the locals to abandon their apathy and throw themselves behind the focal point of their community, Ferguson would drive through the local estates with a loud-hailer urging people to come and support the team. (Brian Clough took a similarly proactive approach at Hartlepool.) Even at this early stage in his managerial career he was developing a reputation as something of a well-meaning autocrat who was not content to restrict his brief to life on the training pitch, the changing room and the dugout. 'If you crossed him or didn't do as you were told, or you let him down, then you were on your way out,' says Gibbons. 'He could be great fun, but you didn't cross Alex Ferguson.'

St Mirren's gates shot up from around 1,000 to nearer five figures during Ferguson's tenure there, but despite his team doing reasonably well on the pitch – considering he was working with a limited budget and a moderate side – he was sacked in 1978. It was the only time in his managerial career that Alex Ferguson has been shown the door – although he came close to it in the early days at United. His dismissal has never been adequately explained, but in a way it is a comfort for all aspiring young managers to know that even the greatest have to fight for success. St Mirren had got rid of a man who would turn out to be one of the greatest managers the game has ever seen – and he quickly showed that his departure was very much the club's loss.

Aberdeen, a bigger club than St Mirren but still without great financial resources compared to Rangers and Celtic, were only too happy to restore Ferguson to full-time employment. After five years' apprenticeship on the hard treadmill of Scottish football, Ferguson had mastered the basics of his profession and was ready to move up a level. His achievements at Aberdeen over the next eight years remain amongst the most impressive in British football history. In a way, given the size of Aberdeen relative to their rivals, they even eclipse what he accomplished at United. Never in living memory had the domination of the Old Firm clubs been broken for so long a period. In the elderly Aberdeen chairman Dick Donald, Ferguson found a kindly, unflappable father figure willing to tolerate and occasionally check the excesses of his young manager's raging ambitions. Donald's son Ian, the club's vice-chairman, recalls how their new acquisition wanted to involve himself in every part of the running of the club – to the mild annoyance of some of the directors, who had told him to concentrate on purely football matters. 'He would say things like: "The bus wasn't right on Saturday, we need more tables and chairs,"' he recalls. 'And then he would go off and see the bus people to sort it out. He was a perfectionist. A 100-miles-an-hour workaholic, always looking to be better than other people.'

Ferguson inherited a solid if unexceptional team that lived, like every other Scottish club, in the shadow of the Old Firm. His players, many of whom have gone into football management and coaching themselves, remember being taken aback by the ferocity and strictness of their thrusting young manager, who had yet to win a single honour in the game. 'Even though he was yet to achieve anything as a manager, he carried an aura about him,' says former striker Eric Black. 'He was a frightening figure and we were in total awe of him. To give an example, I remember once being in a car with him and Willie Miller on the way to training, and my team-mate John Hewitt, who loved fast cars, flashed past us on the outside in a streak of blue. When we got to Pittodrie, Alex stormed into the changing room and flew at John like a screaming dervish. He frightened the life out of him for about ten minutes and then he walked out past the rest of us and gave us a little wink.'

Flying crockery was a common feature of half-time talks in the dressing room. On one occasion, during a European Cup tie, Ferguson, smashed the entire contents of a tea trolley, including the teapot, against the walls. 'I wouldn't say we ever got used to it, but that was his way of expressing frustration or trying to motivate the team,' says Black.

Ferguson could be tough on the more junior players, presumably figuring that the more experienced players were confident enough not to be moved by his outbursts. Central defender Willie Miller, one of the best players of a very good Scottish generation, was a strong enough character to cope with Ferguson, and he had very few confrontations with him. 'My first impression was that he was pretty abrasive and he rubbed two or three players up the wrong way,' says Miller. 'He was a young, very ambitious manager who liked to do things his way. Most of his venom seemed to be directed at the younger players and at times you felt a bit sorry for them, but you knew he was doing it for the benefit of the player and the good of the team. You thought he overstepped the mark sometimes, but most of the players just took the verbal lambasting and then made a joke of it as soon as he had left the room. But he wasn't always domineering in terms of tactics and he would occasionally give a senior player like myself a bit of leeway, just as he does with Roy Keane at United.'

According to Mark McGhee, Ferguson's reputation as a tantrum-thrower of the highest order has tended to obscure the fact that he was a highly intelligent and knowledgeable manager who had a lot more than just that one trick in his book of motivational techniques. 'He's got this reputation of throwing cups around and shouting and giving players the "hair-drier" treatment,' McGhee says, 'but that alone doesn't get respect. After a few cup-throwing sessions you lose people's respect. There was a lot more to him than that as a manager.'

But McGhee admits that even he sometimes found it hard to fathom the curious workings of his manager's mind. 'We were playing Morton, one of my former clubs, and we came in at half-time winning 4-0 and I must have had the ball for thirty of the forty-five minutes,' recalls McGhee. 'I was beating people, putting it through their legs, taking three players on and getting past them all. As I came in I thought he was going to say, "What a fantastic half you've had, Mark", and I was a little surprised when he called me a "greedy bastard" and told me to pass the ball more, saying: "Who do you think you are? Can you not pass the ball?"'

Ferguson knew that the heavy-handed approach didn't work with every player, and that the more insecure characters would crumble rather than rise up and prove him wrong. 'Most of the players could handle him having a mad shouting spree about their performances, but others found it more difficult to cope with the bollockings,' recalls Neale Cooper, a midfielder who, like Miller, McGhee and Black, went into management at the end of his playing career. 'Some of the younger players didn't react in the way he had hoped and their game would fall away. But I think he learned that some players need an arm around the shoulders, while others need a kick up the backside. He was a very, very nice man, always approachable and well mannered, but if he was around the place you could sense it and you'd feel a bit nervous.

'During our half-time talks all the players would sit there leaning forward looking down at the floor and if you looked up and he caught your eye he was straight across: "AND WHAT ABOUT YOU?"' If things weren't going well, he would kick things, he would hit things and he would throw cups. Once he whacked a giant metal flask sitting on a table in middle of the room but it didn't budge because it was full and we knew he'd hurt himself. We were dying to laugh but we just sat there biting our lips.'

Cooper came in for more than the average share of Ferguson furies. He was once made to walk three or four miles on a freezing winter day across Aberdeen to Pittodrie for laughing when one of his team-mates had slipped over in the icy conditions. Cooper, who made his debut for the club at sixteen, bought a flat in Great Western Place in the city centre after establishing himself as a first team regular. 'Not long after moving in I received a call from the manager, who said to me: "I have had a call saying you've been seen coming out of this flat for the last five weeks. Whose is it?" I told him it was mine and he said: "Well get rid of it and go back and live with your mother. You're too young to have your own flat." And put the phone down. So I went back and lived with my mother for two years. I was angry about it at the time, but looking back he was right. I could have got up to no good.'

Cooper also felt his ears warmed when the manager found him holding a glass of vodka and coke after a testimonial match at Tottenham.

Cooper was completely sober, but Ferguson took the glass off him and told him he was going to kill him in training on the Monday. Ferguson never got the chance to carry out his threat because Cooper was away taking his driving test. Instead, he demoted him to the third team reserves for a match away to East Stirlingshire later in the week, after giving him a long lecture on the perils of alcohol. Ferguson was no killjoy and is known to enjoy a glass of wine himself, but he had witnessed at first hand the havoc alcohol had wreaked on the great Rangers player Jim Baxter and he was determined none of his young charges would fall into the same trap.

'Drinking was a no-no,' admits Cooper. 'I always felt nervous even having a shandy in front of him. If you had a bad performance he would always say: "Drinking beer – that's what affects your performance!" If ever the players went out in Aberdeen, he always knew every move we made. He had his spies everywhere.'

After a couple of years building up his team and their confidence, constantly telling them they were better than both Rangers and Celtic, the trophies began to arrive. In 1980 Aberdeen broke the Old Firm's stranglehold and won the championship for the first time since 1955. In total, the club won ten major trophies under Ferguson in a six-year period, including the Scottish Cup (four times), the league title (three times), the League Cup and the European Super Cup. The most famous victory, however, came on a rain-lashed evening in Gothenburg when they caused one of the great upsets of European club football by beating the mighty Real Madrid in the final of the 1983 Cup Winners Cup.

To get to the final, Aberdeen, a team barely known outside the British Isles, had to beat Bayern Munich, the tournament favourites, in the quarter-finals. After a 0-0 draw in Germany they won 3-2 in the home leg after twice coming from behind to record the most glorious victory ever witnessed at Pittodrie stadium. In the build-up to most European matches, Ferguson would go through the strengths of the key players his team were to face, often having flown out to watch the opposition play in the few weeks leading up to the tie. But his approach to the Cup Winners Cup Final was different. 'It was obviously an enormous game and the way Alex played it was not to mention Real Madrid in the whole week before,' recalls Black. 'He didn't go through the opposition saying, "This player's got fifty or a hundred caps for Spain" and so on. It was a clever ploy, because when we went out we felt it was just our eleven against their eleven.'

Aberdeen was virtually deserted as 25,000 fans headed to Sweden on May 11 to see their team take on Alfredo Di Stefano's Real Madrid, Europe's most glamorous and successful club. Real Madrid brought only 3,000 supporters to the Ullevi stadium. 'They didn't bother coming because they thought it was a foregone conclusion,' says Ian Donald. 'As far as they were concerned it was a great Real Madrid side against a bunch of Scottish hicks.'

With world-class players like Stielike, Santillana and Camacho in their side, Madrid began the match as outright favourites, but it was the Scots who went in front after just seven minutes, through Eric Black. The Spaniards quickly pulled a goal back, but any fears that the momentum had swung against the Scots gradually fell away as Aberdeen refused to surrender any of the pitch. As the match went into extra time, Camacho (the future Spanish national manager) was replaced by a player called San José whose first contribution was to punch Mark McGhee in the jaw. McGhee had the last laugh, though, when he sailed past his marker in the 112th minute and delivered a perfect cross for the substitute Hewitt to head the winner.

At the final whistle, Ferguson burst off the bench, only to stumble to the ground and be trampled upon by one of his jubilant colleagues. The squad were mobbed on their return to the north-east of Scotland as tens of thousands from all over the region came out to applaud one of the most remarkable achievements in British football. 'When we flew into Aberdeen airport we could see people actually standing on the airport roof,' remembers Hewitt. 'All the roads were lined with fans right into Aberdeen, down Queens Street to the top end of Union Street, of which you couldn't see an inch because it seemed there were hundreds and thousands of people, some hanging out of windows to greet us. I am Aberdeen born and bred, I've always supported the club, I was a ball boy there and to score the winning goal, well...'

The final, 120 minutes long and played in boggy conditions that only added to the aches in the players' limbs over the days that followed, was an exhausting experience. The emotion of the victory and the ensuing celebrations also took their toll – both physically and in terms of motivation. But a week after the biggest night in the club's history, Ferguson had to lift his men to face Rangers in the final of the Scottish Cup at Hampden Park. 'He certainly fired up his players for the games against Rangers and Celtic,' says John Greig, Rangers' manager in the early 1980s. 'He fired them up against everybody but especially against the Old Firm and he would use every psychological trick in the book to get the best out of his players.'

Aberdeen summoned enough will and physical strength to beat Rangers that afternoon, but it had been a poor game and Ferguson screamed blue murder at them after the match. Nor did he hide his feelings from reporters. 'It was a bit of a shock,' says Black. 'It was not a good performance but hey, we'd won the Cup and the week before that a European trophy. I don't know if there are many other coaches in world football who would have reacted like that, but Alex was always expecting you to move to the next level, and when you got there, it was on to the next one. He hits one Everest and as soon as he's got there he looks for the next one and on he goes.'

The coach journey from Glasgow to the team hotel at St Andrews took place in silence – the manager fuming, the players fretting. But back at the hotel the chairman Dick Donald, embarrassed that his players were so subdued, rose to his feet and urged them to relax and celebrate their achievement. The following day, Ferguson took the rare step of saying sorry to his team. 'His reaction was a surprise to us but to his credit he apologized the next day and admitted he had gone overboard,' says Black. 'But he is the A in "autocrat" and he knows what's required to build a club. And if you know the secret formula, why seek information or dialogue elsewhere? He had a recipe that worked and he stuck to it.

'He was a very bad loser – even if you played him at snooker or table tennis. If we were playing five-a-side in training a ten-minute game would become three and a half hours if his team were losing. (He also had the sharpest elbows at the club.) I remember once at Gordonstoun school, where we used to go for a few days for team building and training, we had organized a cricket match and after spending about three hours getting there, we got all the stumps and kit together and the match finally got underway. Alex was opening the batting and he had only just got to the wicket when Dougie Bell bowled him. He was furious, and after smashing his wicket he cancelled the match and sent us on a run.'

Ferguson's growing success had already attracted the attention of several chairmen south of the border, but after the Cup Winners Cup victory his reputation spread even further. Several leading European clubs – including Barcelona, the biggest of them all – began to sit up and take notice. Ferguson, though, would stay at Aberdeen for three more seasons and take his trophy tally into double figures before the temptation of greater challenges seduced him. Ten trophies in six years at Rangers or Celtic would have been impressive enough, but to have done it with a team of such modest tradition and limited means as Aberdeen made him stand out as a manager of the very highest pedigree.

Arsenal, Celtic, Rangers, Barcelona and Tottenham (to whose overtures he gave serious consideration) all expressed interest before Ferguson finally decided to join Manchester United, the English giants who had spent the previous dozen years living in the shadow of their bitter north-west rivals Liverpool. Not since the days of Sir Matt Busby, another great Scottish manager, in the 1950s and 1960s had the Old Trafford club been able to regard itself as a superpower in English football. As for European glory, United fans could only dream and reminisce.

In Ferguson's final full season at Aberdeen, Scottish football suffered the trauma of seeing the legendary manager Jock Stein collapse during Scotland's World Cup play-off tie against Wales in Cardiff. Ferguson was sitting next to him when the former Celtic manager was taken ill and rushed to hospital. Stein passed away, and Scotland's joy at qualifying for the Mexico finals was almost completely overshadowed by the gloom that hung over the country for months to come. Ferguson took temporary charge of the national side, but the World Cup finals yet again proved to be a failure for the Scots.

• • •

When Ferguson officially took over as manager on 6 November 1986, Manchester United were fourth from bottom of the First Division having won just three of their previous thirteen league games. Moreover, they had recently suffered an humiliating 4-1 home defeat by Southampton in the League Cup. The challenges facing the ambitious young Scot were immense. The club may have been one of the biggest in world football, but at this point their affairs, from top to bottom, were in a state of considerable disarray. His first task was to save them from relegation, and without delving into the transfer market he managed to lift them up the table to the safety of eleventh place by the season's end.

Ferguson slowly set about dismantling the rickety infrastructure of the club and rebuilding it block by block. One of his first priorities was to stamp out the drinking culture that had developed at United, and that meant clashing with the players. Many of the bigger socializers – like Norman Whiteside, Paul McGrath and Bryan Robson – were crowd favourites and established figures at the club, but Ferguson had no qualms in laying down the new law to them. Breaking the booze culture would help in the short-term and it also helped him establish his authority over the players, but Ferguson's vision went far beyond the next few seasons. One of his most important reforms at Old Trafford was to overhaul the youth system, an endeavour that would pay handsome rewards within the next ten years, when the club began to produce players of the calibre of David Beckham, Ryan Giggs, Paul Scholes, Nicky Butt and the Neville brothers – Gary and Phil. Homegrown talent was the best you could get: it was virtually free and it established the players' loyalty to the club as teenagers.

In his first full season, 1987/88, Ferguson brought in Viv Anderson, Steve Bruce and Brian McClair, and United finished the campaign as runners-up. It became obvious the following year, however, when the club finished eleventh again, that there was still a huge reconstruction job facing Ferguson. The following season they continued to struggle, even flirting with relegation for a short while before finishing a lowly thirteenth. The Manchester natives were growing restless. Ferguson had been there for over three years, there were no new trophies in the boardroom cabinet and the team were struggling even for mid-table respectability. To make matters worse, Liverpool remained the dominant force in English football and Arsenal had emerged as their principal rivals. A 5-1 defeat by Manchester City was the final humiliation for many at Old Trafford and the fans began to call for his head. Ferguson has described that period 'as the lowest, most desperate point in all my years in management'. At one match a banner was unfurled that read: 'Three years of excuses, Ta-ra Fergie.'

'I think the job may have taken him a little by surprise, the sheer magnitude of it and the sheer size of the club and also the general state of the club, which was poor – especially the youth set-up, which had become run-down,' says Paul Hince, a reporter with the *Manchester Evening News* who would get to know Ferguson well over the coming years. 'At the time Manchester City were creaming off all the best young players. So he brought in people like Brian Kidd to build that side of it up. It is well documented that some of the players at United liked a drink. There was a clique centred around Norman Whiteside and Paul McGrath and, to a certain extent, Bryan Robson. Robson stayed longer than the other two because Ferguson obviously thought he could still do a job for Manchester United. For a start, he was fit.

'But there was enormous pressure on the board, particularly on [then chairman] Martin Edwards, to dispense with his services. If they hadn't won a trophy that season [1989/90] I don't think there is any doubt they would have got rid of him, because they were mid-table in the league.

'In the *Manchester Evening News* we ran one of those dubious phone-in polls and 83 per cent of callers said Ferguson should be sacked. Most of them were probably Manchester City or Stockport fans – but still. I think it's well documented that in the later years his relationship with Martin Edwards broke down, but I think Alex would be the first to admit that he owes him thanks for sticking by him at the start. In hindsight it was the best thing Edwards ever did, but it took some courage at the time.'

Ferguson almost certainly kept his job due to United's FA Cup run, the crucial moment of which came against Forest in the third round when Mark Robins poached the only goal of the game. 'I think it was that close,' says Hince. 'That's the line between greatness and failure. Ferguson could have been lost to United.' United had played every round away from home, beating Hereford, Newcastle, Sheffield United and Oldham before facing Crystal Palace in the final. After a nerve-wrenching, wildly fluctuating 3-3 draw in their first encounter at Wembley, they won the replay 1-0 thanks to a goal by Lee Martin.

The Cup triumph, a rare day of celebration for the Old Trafford club, gave Ferguson some breathing space. It also gave him some credibility amongst his English critics, who still questioned whether or not his leap from a modest Scottish club to one of the great institutions of English football had been too great for him. The replay also provided stark evidence of Ferguson's ruthlessness when he dropped Scotland goalkeeper Jim Leighton, because he felt his confidence had gone, and replaced him with the relatively unknown Les Sealey. Ferguson's brutality sent a powerful message to United fans that he was not prepared to let sentimentality get in the way of the club's success, and Leighton was just one of many established United players who were to feel the cold blade of Ferguson's axe.

'He is certainly as ruthless a manager as you could wish to meet,' says Hince. 'There is no one – and I mean no one – who was totally safe if Ferguson decided that it was in the interests of Manchester United that they were dropped or sold. He's proved that time and time again.'

Another trophy followed the next season when United beat Barcelona 2-1 in the final of the European Cup Winners Cup, both goals coming from former Barcelona striker Mark Hughes. They also reached the League Cup Final, but the title the club so desperately craved continued to elude them that season and the one following (1991/92), when they appeared to have it in their grasp only to blow it in the final few matches. They were top of the table in mid-April but a 2-0 defeat at Liverpool wrecked their hopes and Leeds United, in only their second season back in the top flight, made a late run on the inside and pipped them at the post.

But twelve months later, the 26-year wait was over. Aided by Frenchman Eric Cantona, who had abandoned Leeds after just six months, United re-established themselves as the country's pre-eminent football club. Cantona had cost just £1.2 million and proved to be one of the most inspired signings in modern football, establishing himself as the fulcrum of the team. Ferguson had made only a passing enquiry about the Frenchman and was amazed to hear Leeds were prepared to let him go. (Goalkeeper Peter Schmeichel, a £500,000 buy from Brondby in Denmark, was an equally significant acquisition a year earlier, the giant Dane bringing an air of authority to the United defence that they had not enjoyed for years.)

The future suddenly looked incandescently bright for United, with a swathe of highly talented youngsters starting to make a name for themselves in the youth teams and pushing their way into contention for places in the senior side. Within a few years Giggs, Beckham, Scholes, the Neville Brothers and Butt would all be regulars in the United side, as well as established internationals. The championship triumph made Ferguson the first manager to win the league title on both sides of the border. He was named Manager of the Year, and United stood at the threshold of the most successful period in their history.

In a way, the hard work had been done. Ferguson had survived the early criticism and lack of success. He had overhauled the club's 'substructure'. He had removed the players he felt were a bad influence. He had bought well. He was about to reap the fruits of his youth policy. Confidence had grown with two cup victories and then rocketed when the title was reclaimed, and Ferguson had established his authority in both the changing room and the board room. 'Winning the Cup saved Ferguson's career, but winning the title was the turning point for United because from there they turned from a big club into a global monster,' says Hince.

The following season United swept to the double, missing out on what would have been an historic 'treble' when they were beaten 3-1 in the League Cup Final by Aston Villa. For a while that season it looked as if they had blown the title when Blackburn reduced a sixteen-point lead to only goal difference, as a string of suspensions threatened to wreck United's challenge. United regrouped, fought back, and took the crown with eight points to spare before thrashing Chelsea 4-0 in the FA Cup Final.

Expectations of more United glory were high at the start of 1994/95 season. Andy Cole had arrived for £7 million from rivals Newcastle, but in January, at a crucial moment in the campaign, Cantona – who had just been sent off – jumped into the crowd at Selhurst Park and attacked a Crystal Palace fan. The incident caused a sensation, dominating the headlines and distracting the club from its business on the pitch. The Frenchman was charged, convicted, ordered to carry out 120 hours of community service and banned from football for seven months. It was a difficult period for United and Ferguson's diplomatic skills were severely tested, both in his dealings with the Frenchman and with the United board of directors, some of whom were keen to see the back of a player they regarded as a liability who could damage the commercial image of the club.

Ferguson, though, knew Cantona was invaluable to the team and stood by him throughout the ordeal, even flying to Paris to persuade him to return when the Frenchman was in two minds about his future. Cantona and the board both succumbed. 'If you speak to any of his players they will tell you that if they've got any problems, soccer problems or personal or marital difficulties, they go and see him,' says Hince. 'His door is never shut.'

Ferguson was growing in confidence and authority by the season, something that was reflected in the way he treated the press. At the beginning, when his job was on the line, he rarely treated journalists to what Old Trafford's regular reporters call the 'hair-drier' treatment. But as the trophies rolled in and the coffers overflowed, Ferguson became increasingly aloof towards the press and often downright hostile and intimidating – because he could afford to. His position was safe at Old Trafford and he was able to bully critical journalists with impunity. If they continued to be critical, he simply wouldn't recognize their existence. If you were a journalist whose beat was Manchester United, then access to the governor – or at least amiable relations with him – was vital in the interests of the newspaper.

'You never get a one to one with Alex Ferguson,' says journalist Ian McGarry. 'It's all dependent on his mood. He can be the most charming, funny raconteur on some occasions, and other times he can be surly, unhelpful, indignant and very, very indifferent to the press. If he's angry, most of the time he treats you with indifference. He will ignore you or he will be very patronizing, which can be very intimidating. He has developed such a huge reputation and has so many avenues of influence throughout the game, that people are genuinely scared to get on the wrong side of him. Including journalists.'

Working for the local *Manchester Evening News*, Paul Hince often found himself walking through a minefield with the United manager, torn between keeping himself in Ferguson's favour while trying to write objective, informative pieces. 'He may have been worried about upsetting the press in the early days, but he certainly hasn't been since then,' says Hince. 'For the first few years when it was a bit sticky for him, perhaps he needed a few friends in the press... but certainly not after about five or six years, when he had become bombproof.

'I wrote up a fairly innocuous interview with him once in which I speculated that he might go if he won the Champions League, as he would then have a full set of trophies. It's very dangerous at a club like Manchester United to start rumours like that, because shareholders get nervous and money gets wiped off the stock exchange, and I was treated to one of his famous hair-drier blasts down the phone. He was blazingly angry. It was one expletive after another and the earpiece was melting. He finished the conversation by saying "And don't f**king speak to me again!" And slammed the phone down.'

According to Eric Black, Ferguson's treatment of the press had changed little from his earliest days at Aberdeen. 'I wouldn't say he bullies the press, but I think he's very clever in manipulating them to his advantage,' says Black. 'I don't think it's off the cuff. I think that, like everything he does, there's a plan and a strategy behind it.'

Many journalists found Ferguson's often haughty and unhelpful attitude to the press astonishing. 'In the United States, players and officials get fined if they don't talk to the media,' says Gabriele Marcotti, a London-based Italian journalist. 'Here you have the most commercial club around, Manchester United, with a manager who rules with an iron fist, treats his players like children and doesn't let them talk to the media.'

• • •

United finished the 1994/95 season without a trophy. Kenny Dalglish's Blackburn pipped them to the title and Everton beat them 1-0 in the FA Cup Final at Wembley. In the summer, Ferguson once again showed his cold-blooded, unsentimental approach to running United's team affairs when he offloaded three of his best players: Mark Hughes, Paul Ince and Andrei Kanchelskis. Question marks were raised over Ferguson's judgement, particularly as Eric Cantona would not return from his ban until two months into the season. Some fans protested against the departure of Hughes, an Old Trafford idol, but Ferguson's estimation that the Welshman's best years were behind him proved to be more or less accurate, although he would continue to play in the top flight at Chelsea.

The sale of Ince was even more baffling to the outside world, as the England midfielder appeared to be near the peak of his game. Ince, a man who liked to refer to himself as The Governor, was as stunned as anyone at Old Trafford by the news he was going to be sold on. Those who have devoted much of their working life to studying Ferguson's actions came to the conclusion that Ince had simply got too big for his boots as far as Ferguson was concerned. 'When I heard Ince turned up in the car park for training in a new car with the number plate GUV 1, I thought, "Well, Incey, that really is a bad career move when you have

Ferguson as your boss",' says Hince. "'You won't be at Old Trafford too much longer." And of course, he wasn't.

'If he thinks it's for the good of Manchester United, then Ferguson will sell anyone. There is never any sentimentality. Six months before Cantona announced his retirement [at the end of the 1996/97 season], Ferguson told me he was finished as a top-class player. Fergie knew that he had lost whatever spark or edge he had. Cantona was a fanatical trainer but his weight didn't look right at the end. He'd stopped flogging himself in training, which he had to do as a big lad, so when Cantona said he wanted to retire, Fergie accepted it immediately. He knew already that he was gone.'

Ferguson showed at Aberdeen that he was never afraid to give youngsters their chance. As a sixteen-year-old straight out of school, Neale Cooper found himself playing against Celtic in front of 60,000 fans at Parkhead. At United, Ferguson took an even bigger gamble when he placed his faith in the club's emerging youngsters – five of the regulars were twenty-one or under – and many experts felt he had made the first serious strategic mistake of his time at Old Trafford. 'You'll win nothing with kids,' former Liverpool defender Alan Hansen told *Match of the Day* viewers at the start of the season. But once again Ferguson's horse trader's gut instinct was proved right, his ruthlessness justified, as 'Fergie's Fledglings' swept to an historic 'double double'.

In Ferguson's tenth year in charge, United defended their league title after overhauling Newcastle's fourteen-point lead at Christmas. For most commentators, the season's turning point came when Newcastle's manager Kevin Keegan lost his temper live on television in response to provocative comments made by Ferguson. Keegan's outburst was seen as evidence of the Scotsman's ability to intimidate people – even at long range. By now, Ferguson, United's longest serving manager since the great Sir Matt Busby, had established himself as one of the best managers in world football, and one of the most successful in the history of British football. But one trophy still eluded him – the European Cup. It would continue to do so the following season, when United finished the campaign empty-handed as Arsenal swept to the double in Arsène Wenger's first full season in charge as manager.

United returned with a vengeance, strengthening their defence with the acquisition of Dutch defender Jaap Stam and sharpening the attack with the addition of Dwight Yorke. In one of the most exciting climaxes to an English season in recent years, United recorded a remarkable treble of victories in the league, FA Cup and Champions League. The European final in Barcelona's Nou Camp turned out to be one of the most extraordinary in the history of the competition, as United scored two goals in stoppage time to beat Bayern Munich 2-1. The 31-year quest for their second European crown – on what would have been Sir Matt Busby's ninetieth birthday – was finally over.

'Bayern were very much better for about seventy minutes of the match, but there were two reasons why United won it,' argues football and financial writer Simon Kuper. 'First, was Ferguson's decision to keep on these killer subs, [Teddy] Sheringham and Solskjaer, when many other clubs would let them go because they're paying a lot of money and they're not in the team. And, of course, they both came on and scored. The other reason is that United have always had this incredible attitude. People say it's luck when you score in the last two minutes, but it isn't. Germany always used to do it. Certain teams do it. Winners score in the last minute. You're completely gone, you've gone ninety minutes, you're hurting, you've pulled a hamstring, you've been kicked to pieces but you keep going. So in terms of character, that last minute defines United – Ferguson's United.'

Although Bayern were the better side on the night, many felt that United deserved to win Europe's premier club competition for their overall performance in the earlier rounds. 'I think the 3-2 victory over Juventus, after being two goals down, was probably the finest display by any English team in Europe in the last twenty years, including Liverpool's triumphs,' says Ian McGarry. 'For that alone, people would argue United deserved to win the European Cup that season.'

The European triumph also gave Ferguson the credibility he had always craved amongst the Continent's top coaches, who had traditionally taken a dim view of the qualities of British football managers. 'British managers have long been a bit of a joke on the Continent, but Ferguson single-handedly changed all that,' says Kuper.

Ferguson, who became a knight of the realm in 1999, had now won every significant trophy available, but although United retained their Premier League titles over the next two seasons – making it seven triumphs in nine seasons – they were unable to repeat their success in Europe.

There were whispers that Ferguson's hunger for success might have been dulled, having secured his reputation as the country's most successful manager and with his projected retirement date fast approaching. Two incidents, however, proved that the fires of his burning ambitions had not faded. The first was in his treatment of David Beckham, England's most popular footballer, one of the biggest celebrities in the world and an idol of the Old Trafford faithful. With his wife away on business, Beckham called the United training ground to say that their son Brooklyn was sick and that he was going to stay at home to look after him. Ferguson's response was to punish Beckham by dropping the midfielder for United's next game against Leeds. 'I thought it was appalling, and I thought Beckham was totally justified in that incident,' says Gabriele Marcotti. 'But I think Ferguson knew he had the media in his pocket and he knew he could get away with laying down the law and saying no one's bigger than the club, not even a sick child. The message to Beckham was "I am your master, bow down before the one you serve."'

Ferguson did get away with it, although there was credible speculation in the press for several weeks that the United manager had pushed the Beckhams too far and that his most valuable asset wanted to leave the club he had joined as a young teenager and pursue his career abroad. For Ian McGarry, the incident was a vivid illustration of Ferguson's traditional working-class values, honed during his uncompromising upbringing in Glasgow. 'I think Alex probably went back to his cultural background in that instance, saying that if your baby's sick your missus should be at home looking after it. Not you. You've got a job to do. It was a very old-fashioned, stereotypical male-orientated view of family life and it didn't go down too well with David and Victoria. For a few weeks there was real concern that this might be too much for Beckham and he would ask for a transfer. It almost brought about the end.'

The second episode involved the Dutch defender Jaap Stam, by most experts' estimations one of the very best defenders in the world over the previous few seasons. Stam could not have been happier at United and felt so at home in the north of England and his mock-Tudor mansion that he had even developed a Mancunian accent.

But three days after ordering himself a brand new kitchen, the news broke that he had been sold to Lazio in Italy. It so happened that he had just published his autobiography and the press had seized on one or two quotes – from an otherwise uncontroversial read – that appeared to besmirch the reputation of Ferguson, whom Stam said had approached him when he was still under contract with PSV Eindhoven. He also said something to the effect that Beckham would probably never win *Mastermind* and described the Neville brothers as 'whingers' known in the dressing room as 'busy c**ts'. You can imagine Ferguson giving the big Dutchman an early morning roasting in his training ground, but the comments hardly added up to a sackable offence. And besides, Stam spent the rest of the book telling the reader how much he loved United and worshipped Ferguson. It was all very curious, but after a few weeks the general consensus amongst those who had been sniffing around Old Trafford – and Stam – in search of the truth behind his brutal axing turned out be far more prosaic. Ferguson, unlike almost everybody else in the business, didn't think he was the right type of player. The United manager had been hoping that the physically intimidating Dutchman would also develop an imposing moral stature. He wanted Stam to lead the back line with more authority, to teach and cajole the younger players into a stronger unit. But Ferguson had slowly realized that this was never going to happen and that for all his other qualities, Stam was a quiet character lacking the presence of a central defender such as Arsenal's Tony Adams.

'He was furious about some of the things he wrote, but he wouldn't have sold him for that reason alone,' says Hince. 'He had spotted something in Stam. If Alex Ferguson thought that Jaap Stam could help Manchester United win the Premiership or the Champions League, there's no way in the world he would have sold him. Stam could have called him a bastard in his book, but he still wouldn't have sold him. It was the same when he sold Mark Hughes, a huge hero at Old Trafford – no sentimentality.'

Simon Kuper, an expert on Dutch football who has interviewed most of the country's leading players, says the timing of Stam's autobiography was a coincidence and merely distracted the press from the real issue. 'Ferguson had been trying to get rid of Stam for months and the opportunity came along because Laurent Blanc had become available [at Inter Milan]. As it happened, at that time Stam wrote a book that didn't serve his cause very well, but that's an entirely irrelevant detail.

'Stam was stunned. At United everyone loves you, everyone stands up for you. There is an attitude that we're all in this together and that's why we are so strong. If there is a punch-up on the field, Roy Keane will be the first to help you. If the press criticizes you, Ferguson will scream the head off the journalist who wrote it. So when the man at the centre of this, Ferguson, says, "Right, you're out of here", it's an unbearable shock. You've been kicked out of the communal kindergarten.

'Stam came from the Dutch tradition where as soon as the manager starts to brief them, the players say, "Yeah, but..." At United it's the opposite. The players see Ferguson as a sort of mix between a demi-god and a headmaster who will cane you. Ferguson does it verbally, although perhaps he's actually caned players – I don't know, but it would be a good tabloid story. He's untouchable and the players live in dread and admiration. He's like an Old Testament God to them.'

After Stam's departure early in the 2001/02 season, it was Ferguson's relationship with England captain Beckham that captivated the press. By early February, after eight months of negotiations, the £40 million-rated midfielder had still failed to put his pen to a new contract. Rumours abounded that the club would be happy to cash in on him before he became worth nothing under the Bosman ruling once his original deal had expired. To the outside world, it seemed that United – as represented by Ferguson – and Beckham were playing a game of cat-and-mouse, and the manager was taking every opportunity to remind his player of his unofficial motto that no player was more important the club. Beckham's standing in English football had soared after a string of inspirational displays as national captain and his goal in the ninety-fourth minute of a 2-2 draw against Greece secured England's place in the World Cup finals and made him an object of even greater national admiration.

Four days later, United went to Athens for a Champions League match against Olympiakos that they needed to win after a defeat by Deportivo Coruna. They needed to field their strongest possible team, but on the eve of the match Ferguson dropped his bombshell. 'At a press conference Ferguson said he was dropping Beckham, but at a later conference with television cameras present he said nothing of the sort,' says Hince. 'What Ferguson wanted was headlines on the back pages, knowing Beckham's wife, his father and his friends would call him that morning and say, "Jesus Christ you're dropped, what's going on?" Knowing this, Ferguson, as I understand it, went up to Beckham at the training session that morning and said something to the effect of, "You've had a really emotionally and physically draining weekend. Do you think you're up for tonight?" knowing full well that Beckham would be enraged and say, "Of course I'm up for it. I'll show you." Beckham, of course, scores the first goal and has a great game. This was Ferguson at his wiliest.'

Ken Gallacher believes Ferguson's dictatorial, often provocative, treatment of his players is part of a strategy to maintain their desire for more success. 'It must be very difficult to motivate players earning £50,000 a week. It dulls the appetite for victory knowing that you are that comfortable,' he says.

Ian McGarry believes Ferguson is harder on himself than anyone and when he comes down on his players he is doing no more than asking them to live up to the same exacting standards he has set for himself. 'He demands the same amount of obsession he has. Every year people say United cannot lift themselves because the hunger has gone, they've won everything. But they keep coming back and doing it again. Each time a new season begins, something demonic in him pours out and infects the players. They've got professional pride but he's the one with the hunger.'

In twenty-eight years of management, Ferguson has demanded absolute obedience from his players, but there has always been method in his military manner. A hard taskmaster on the training ground and in the changing room, he has dominated his troops with the unshakable conviction that they will only triumph if they are well-drilled, submissive and united under his command. He understood from the outset that you do not become one of the most revered managers in world football by being sensitive.

For all the rigid discipline he imposes on his players, Ferguson dotes on them and never criticizes them in public. 'He takes as much pleasure in the development of his players' characters, if he's had them from a young age, as he does in them as footballers,' says Gibbons. 'I would say that one of the things he will be most proud of in his career will have been helping these boys grow up to become what you would call "fine men", reliable and trustworthy, no scallywags.'

In his private life, by all accounts, Ferguson shows the same unwavering loyalty to his friends as he does to his players, but also a gentleness and humility rarely seen in public. 'He's got a devotion to friends and family that's almost Sicilian,' says Glen Gibbons. 'He invited me to have dinner with him in Glasgow not long ago and when I arrived he was sitting there with three guys who he was at primary school with. He had remained friends with them for over fifty years. It's the same with his family. He's very, very, very tight on family.' Ferguson's European and domestic rivals privately rubbed their hands with glee when the Scotsman announced that he would be retiring as Manchester United's manager at the end of the 2001/2002 season. When Busby, the last great United manager, retired at the start of the 1970s, the 1968 European Cup winners went into a sharp decline that led to their relegation in 1974 and then a long period of relative mediocrity.

However, in February 2002, United fans – and shareholders – were rejoicing and their rivals were despairing at the announcement that sixty year-old Ferguson, encouraged by his family, had made a U-turn and decided to stay on in his post. You could almost hear the groans in London, Leeds and Liverpool. As he entered into negotiations, Ferguson knew that he could virtually write his own cheque for a new deal, as United's six-month search for a replacement manager had drawn a blank. A number of candidates were linked with the post, including Celtic's Martin O'Neill, Leeds United's David O'Leary, Bayern Munich's Ottmar Hitzfeld, AS Roma's Fabio Capello, Arsenal's Arsene Wenger and England coach Sven Goran Eriksson – in fact, just about every leading manager in European football. Ultimately, however, the only character big enough to sit in Alex Ferguson's seat was sitting in it already, a part of the Old Trafford furniture. Ferguson, they discovered, really is irreplaceable.

INDEX